BOXCAR TO BOARD ROOMS

MANNIE JACKSON

ISBN: 0615598250
ISBN-13: 978-0-615-59825-3

In memory of my mother Margaret and father Emmett.

You will always be an important part of my life.

Thank you, and I send my love.

In The Beginning...

ALL PROCEEDS FROM THE SALE OF THIS BOOK WILL
BENEFIT CANCER RESEARCH AND THE I-LEAP ACADEMIC
SCHOLARSHIP PROGRAM.

FOREWORD

In my life and travels I haven't always remembered what people I have met said, or for that matter exactly what they did; but I never forget how they made me feel. This book was written in the hope that it will make you feel good about the potential of the human spirit and that you never stop pursuing your dreams.

-Mannie Jackson

A FEW OF MY FAVORITE QUOTES

"My purpose in life is driven by the fact that I don't want anyone, Black or White, to be treated the way I have been treated."

Nelson Mandela

"I learned to chase my dreams and to always believe."

Coach Joe Lucco

"There's a beautiful girl and a good athlete in every city in the country. Don't get caught up."

My grandfather, S.B. Jackson

"If you've given the appearance or are suspected of being dishonest or unethical, consider yourself to have failed."

Ed Spencer

"Management is about order and control. Leadership is about making changes and achieving goals."

Joe White, President, University of Illinois

"A great thing about American society is that few of us are very far from humble beginnings."

Joe White, President, University of Illinois

"No matter what home you are in or its condition, it represents a step up for someone."

Grandma Lois White

"One's attitude versus aptitude will determine one's altitude in life."

Reverend Jesse L. Jackson Jr.

"Don't miss out on all the good waiting for the best."

Luther Vandross

"Adversity reveals genius."

Horace

"The block of granite which was an obstacle in the path of the weak becomes a stepping stone in the path of the strong."

Thomas Carlyle

"Ninety-nine days of love and devotion is squandered in ten seconds with a foul tone or misspoken word."

Unknown

CONTENTS

MANNIE JACKSON

PRAISE FOR THE AUTHOR

"Mannie Jackson is the perfect guide to teach how to convert dreams to reality. Like President Lincoln and other Americans who rose high from humble beginnings, Mannie has been there, done that, and now he tells us how to do it too."

B. Joseph White, President Emeritus, University of Illinois

"What I most admire about Mannie is his great success and his enthusiastic willingness to share his success through philanthropy. He is an outstanding example of 'those who earn it should share it with others.' I firmly believe in the mantra itself and support Mannie for carrying it out."

Edson W. Spencer, Former Honeywell Chairman and CEO

"Winning was what it was all about. Mannie is my lifelong friend and his achievements in the business world and life in general are beyond written description. 'Jack,' as I call him, always reaches for perfection and more often than not achieves excellence."

Govoner Vaughn, Retired Executive, Detroit Edison

Director of Alumni Relations for the Harlem Globetrotters

"Mannie Jackson was then, and throughout his career, a leader. Yes, he had great athletic talent... but he drove himself to excel. (He was) a hard worker who led by example."

Dennis Swanson, Executive Director NBC Affiliate, New York City

Past President ESPN and Wide World of Sports

"In the more than 10 years that I was a silent partner of Mannie's in the Harlem Globetrotters, we did not have one acrimonious or disagreeable moment (a rare thing in business these days)... Mannie provided the truly inspirational leadership that transformed the Harlem Globetrotters from a marginal organization to a very successful and profitable franchise business. Importantly, he achieved the transformation with a sense of integrity that is rare and was truly remarkable. It has been my honor and privilege to have been Mannie's friend and business partner for many years. His accomplishments are indeed legendary."

Dennis Mathisen, President, Marshall Group

"I had the privilege of meeting and getting to know Mannie Jackson at the University of Illinois....[His] has been a remarkable journey for someone who climbed the ladder in an extraordinary fashion. His philanthropy is unquestioned and his commitment to his causes is unmatched. All coming from someone who started with so little. Our personal journey covers over 50 years and it has been my personal privilege to call him a friend of whom I am very proud."

Jerry Colangelo, President, USA Basketball, President of JHC Partnership

Former Owner/President of Phoenix Suns

Former Owner/President of Arizona Diamondbacks

ACKNOWLEDGMENTS

It seems to me that the engines that drive optimism, hope and human spirit are in short supply these days. I started on this book years ago when I was first struck by this feeling. I thought a world seemingly proliferated with negative political campaigning, racism, job losses and foreclosures, would value hearing an unfiltered accounting of a triumph of the human spirit against a backdrop of poverty and intolerance. My life story, as famed writer Stephen King says, is a plot-less first hand saga of a child born in a rail way boxcar who traveled the world captaining one of the greatest brands of all of times. I thought by sharing my unlikely journey – "born in a railway boxcar to life in corporate boardrooms" – a few of you, or maybe even just one person, would receive inspiration or renewed hope and make these efforts worthwhile.

In 1991, during my drive for an NBA franchise, sports writer Tom Cushman had a major impact on my looking back over my life. Together we drafted a book proposal that regrettably failed to meet the standards of my then-agent, the William Morris Agency, and 12 A-list publishing houses. Each had concerns about the writing, but responded with letters encouraging us not to give up on the story. My thanks go out to Tom and especially all those publishing companies. It's because of them that I wasn't about to give up. As writer Stephen King says, though I paraphrase, "Editors and publishers themselves have all sinned and fallen short of perfection, thus are not divine." Had I listened to all the naysayers in my life, I might still be shining shoes at Sunset Hills Country Club. Nonetheless, thank you William Morris Agency, all the well-intentioned publishing houses, and my old friend

Tom Cushman, a truly great writer. In many ways, Tom, this book will be for you.

Writing this book, I've relied on memory and media research for a period spanning seven decades. Many of those who influenced me the most, who shared in my early struggles, and who believed in me while knowing I was a long-odds project have now passed on, yet I felt their presence as I remembered their gifts. In recent years I've become deeply appreciative of spiritual forces, as well as the science of intuition and the powers of prayer and meditation.

I am deeply indebted and grateful to my wife Catherine, my adopted son Randall, my daughters Candace and Cassandra, my sister Marjorie, my brother Steve, and all my extended family members. My wife and family have been the single most important forces in my life. I've also had many colleagues and co-workers over the years who have helped immensely along the way. Their support and contributions have not been forgotten, nor are they unappreciated.

My hometown often takes a beating in my memories and dreams because of its history of prejudice, ignorance and injustices. Although social activist Randall Robinson is fond of saying bad social conditions almost always produce bad results, I was a fortunate one and I have arrived at a place of balance by recalling the good times and the many good people like Joe Lucco, Dick Hutton, Nina Baird, Margo Kreige, Spike Riley, Bob Wetzel, Bob and Chuck Richards, Delores Penelton, Herman Shaw, Bill Penelton, my teachers Ms. Moomaw and Ms. Edwards, Govoner Vaughn, Dr. Hightower, Mayor Neibur and others in that small, Midwestern, southern Illinois town who have given their unconditional support and encouragement.

Thanks to my collaborative editor Arlene Matthews, who has proven to be the best thing that happened to this project when, after a year of missed deadlines and false starts, it was about to be scrapped for a second time. Arlene has proven to be smart, professional, focused and honest. She seems to always stay on task: no distractions or excuses. Arlene edited my story, as I hope she does every writing project I do in the future. We make a good team.

To my cover designer and marketer Steve Fischer of Redline Dezign, thanks for always indulging me and my creative juices. To Colleen Lenihan Olson and Eve Miner of the Harlem Globetrotters, thanks for chasing down all the staff members and data I needed to meet deadlines. To my friend Dr. John Watson and his wife Sue, I wanted so badly for John and I to both recount the details of the unusual Black-and-White story of our friendship.

And finally to my dad Emmett, who died June 23, 2011 at age 91 and insisted I not give up the book idea – as he knew in detail almost every story I tell in this book and would often interrupt me and finish a sentence or thought about my life story and events: I love you Dad, and thanks. The book is finally done. Enjoy.

INTRODUCTION

What a great day May 11, 2008 was in Champaign, Illinois. I just finished an abundant 2,000-calorie Midwest-style breakfast with my wife Cathy and our two daughters, and I remember feeling as if all sounds had been put on "mute" as I looked around at a collage of college memories. In about one hour, at 9:30 a.m., I would receive an Honorary Doctorate of Humane Letters from my alma mater. I'd walk among a procession of over 4,000 college seniors, graduate students, deans, chancellors and department heads toward the University of Illinois Assembly Hall and the most improbable appearance – and just maybe the proudest moment – of my life.

Stephanie Lulay of the local morning newspaper wrote, "Mannie Jackson, a U. of I. alumnus, to speak at the University's 137th Commencement today. Jackson, a former member and team captain of the Illini basketball team, has served on the boards of directors of six Fortune 500 companies. He is a founder and past chairman of the Executive Leadership Council, and current Chairman of the Naismith Memorial Basketball Hall of Fame. A former player for the Harlem Globetrotters, he has been the Globetrotters' owner and Chairman since 1993." I remember smiling to myself and thinking, *not a mention of my being African-American or being born in a railroad boxcar.* I'm guessing that maybe at her age she doesn't know about boxcars, or maybe to her it mattered less where I came from than where I am today.

On this cool May morning amid a slight drizzle from the overcast sky, I also remember having so much chatter going on in my brain, it was hard to focus. It was hard for me to appreciate all the well wishes. It was hard to remember my mom Margaret and dad Emmett and harder still to recognize all the old friendships; it was regrettably difficult to give my wife and proud family the focus and attention they deserved as they shared this honor. I do remember the four thoughts that were pounding in my head. First, 137 years ago would have been just eight years after the Emancipation Proclamation, and there were certainly no Black commencement speakers in this green room in those days. Second, I mustn't neglect to thank University Vice President Bill Sturtevant for his kind words and Chancellor Richard Herman for his introduction. Third, I must acknowledge University President Joe White and our friendship – along with the leap of faith he took in inviting me to speak before this large graduating class. No matter what other impressions you take away from reading this book, attending college and graduating from the University of Illinois was the single most important decision I've ever made. The fourth thought I couldn't shake was, *How did I get here? How did I get so fortunate?* Because by any measure, it's been an amazing road traveled that has allowed me to come this far from the humblest of origins.

I was born in Illmo, Missouri and raised in my grandfather Jackson's adopted home state of Illinois, which was still shackled by segregation at every turn: in its schools, public accommodations, voting booths, and every place where whites would receive an advantage and where it served their interest to keep Black folks down and separated as a hapless underclass. There were no gray areas in those days: If you were non-white, and particularly if you were Black, you caught hell any time you crossed that cruel and rigid line of racial demarcation. Yet, over the course of my life, I was able to move from high school and college basketball to around-the-world travels with the Harlem

Globetrotters into a notable 25-year corporate career in which I was one of the very first African-Americans to break through the glass ceiling into executive management. Inside ever-sacred Fortune 500 boardrooms, I was able to work alongside some of the world's most powerful movers and shakers overseeing Ashland, Reebok, Stanley/Black and Decker, Jostens, General Motors and Honeywell. I also led and participated in several successful mainstream entrepreneurial ventures, including ownership of one of the premier brands in the world: the Harlem Globetrotters.

All of this has resulted in this book: a collection of lessons learned, of survival techniques, and of tales of incredible "Forrest Gump-like" encounters with everyone from presidents and heads of state of over 100 countries to many of the other celebrated luminaries of our time – including Pope John Paul II, Prince Charles, Nelson Mandela, Fidel Castro, Oprah Winfrey, Barack Obama, Colin Powell, Bill Clinton, Dr. Martin Luther King, Rev. Jessie L. Jackson, Ronald Reagan, George Bush, Jimmy Carter, Walter Mondale, the Dalai Lama, and scores of others. I've rang the New York Stock Exchange opening or closing bell four times – and would you believe those four times were *in a 90-day period?*

I am writing this book because it occurred to me that telling what I've learned – and particularly sharing the formula used to turn the Globetrotters around – could be a way to help others. I do believe I've actually turned my boyhood dreams into reality against all the seemingly insurmountable odds. How? And why me? These are questions I really can't answer alone. How much of it was will, how much was skill, and how much "karma" or destiny? I don't know, but all along the way many talented and generous people of all backgrounds guided me at every step in my journey. A good friend would always say to me in a most respectful way, "'Jumpin Jack,' you've always been lucky." I'd think to myself, *maybe so*. But it's also true I've worked hard to cash a lot of "long odds" chips at the poker table of life and allowed myself to learn so much from people from all walks of life. Their knowledge and inspiration are among the things that I want to pass along.

Ironically, for all my mathematically improbable accomplishments, this book project has been one of the most challenging, most time-consuming and most enjoyable things I have ever undertaken. This book was actually started back in the early 1990s through the inspiration of my friend, San Diego sports editor Tom Cushman. It has been written, rewritten, shelved intermittently, and then reincarnated with a somewhat different vision than the one with which I began. During the course of writing it, my life continued to grow and evolve. I've become comfortable not being a celebrity or household name. The media has never been addicted to covering my personal profile; therefore, my leadership roles and world travels have most often gone under the public radar. After 40-plus years of working, traveling to over 100 countries, and studying under scores of great mentors, I am ready to finalize this version of my improbable life story, which you'll find to be part memoirs, part educational, and hopefully part inspirational. As I finally conclude this effort, part of me is actually sorry to let it go. I'll let you, readers, solve the question of how I rose so far from so little.

The writing and researching has been a form of time travel for me. During it, I encountered many of the people who have meant the most to me: family, teachers, friends, mentors. And though some are no longer living – in the literal sense – our meetings have been as "real," as weird, and as meaningful as they have sometimes been mystical. There have been times when I felt transported. As an example, late one night, sitting in my office in Arizona tapping out a scene on my laptop, I suddenly found myself back on the streets of Harlem in 1962 standing outside of Small's Paradise Lounge a few blocks from the now-fabled Apollo Theater at 3:00 a.m. There I was: this young man living big in the biggest city in the world, with so many choices, all dressed up in a custom-made designer suit, with a luxury car, a bank account and the notoriety of a performing athlete, figuring out where to go... because at 21, with what lay ahead, my life and my party was just getting started. I remembered – no, I experienced – the feel of the clothes I was wearing; I could smell the smoke of seared barbecue and grease from the fresh fried chicken. And it all seemed to blend perfectly with the blues and soul music in the background and the breezes of that great city. As I experienced this part of the book I was young again. It was a long while before I "came to" and realized that more than a half century had passed. Who knew that writing could do this to a man?

But for all its magic, the process of writing is just a means to an end. The story is not complete until it is told. And so, reader, I'm offering you my improbable story. I hope it will engage you and entertain you, but mostly I hope it will inspire you to listen to and believe in your own dreams.

The closing of my 2008 commencement speech at the University of Illinois began: "You are indeed blessed to live in a free and open society on a planet that is hurling through this mysterious universe at an incredible speed. You have no control over the speed or the destination. Find your unique happiness, find something and someone you can become passionate about and sit back, share your space peacefully and enjoy the journey." Reader, I say those words again today, this time to you. And remember, dreams do come.

1 A FAMILY OF DREAMERS

In name, the town of Illmo, Missouri no longer exists. Located on the Mississippi River, approximately 130 miles south of St. Louis, it was at one time known as Illmo-Fornfelt, a merging of two small, inconspicuous southern farm communities. But today, all that remains of that identity is the lettering on decaying buildings. The residue of Illmo-Fornfelt has been re-christened Scott City. Recently, the region's focal point has shifted to Cape Girardeau, Missouri. Eight miles to the north, it's the town that produced conservative icon Rush Limbaugh.

Illmo was both a river town and a railroad town. It was there I was born to Emmett Leo Jackson, a 19-year-old for whom you turned your head twice so as not to mistake this proud colored boy for being white or Mexican. He was tall, lean and talked about as the handsome and sharp-minded Navy man who married Margaret Louise White, a very dark-skinned, well-dressed, beautiful woman with a bigger-than-life smile. She was a seamstress and clothing designer who worked as a day laborer and domestic worker for middle-class white families. The couple attracted attention from all races and together they made an oddly model couple. (Most of these words were written by my Dad's oldest sister following her first meeting with her future sister-in-law.)

I came into this world in a Cotton Belt Railroad boxcar. My maternal grandfather, Alonzo "Lonnie" White, was a so-called "straw boss," or foreman's assistant, for the Cotton Belt. It was hard, lonely and dangerous work, supervising a maintenance and repair crew of 20 other Black workers and traveling up and down miles of track via hand-propelled trolleys or on foot. He never complained because, first and foremost, he had a job and also because he had the ability to endow his work with a sense of noble purpose. He was recognized as a leader, a gifted baseball player and a natural pianist who could play any piece, especially jazz or blues, by ear. But the railroad paid the bills, and one of Lonnie's perks was a genuine railroad boxcar in which to house his family.

The boxcar we called home stood on cinder blocks a foot off the ground with three or four wooden stairs leading up to a make-shift entry. Once inside, it was compartmentalized with bed sheets, plywood and draperies in order to accommodate our blended family and provide a little bit of privacy. There were about a dozen of us living there at any one time. This included my mother and I (my father was only rarely home on leave), Grandpa Lonnie and Grandma Lois, several of my mother's brothers, and her sister, my Aunt Dee. As our family expanded (my sister Marjorie came along two years after me, and some cousins were added to the mix), a second boxcar was added to form an "L" shape. Lonnie built a plywood wall between the two boxcars, with a door enabling the family to go back and forth between the two.

Our boxcar "complex" had a great room that served as both the kitchen and adult bedroom. The common toilet was 100 yards away down a dark path that followed a creek into the woods. Sometimes my older uncles would tell scary stories about who or what might be lurking in those woods, and it made you think twice about whether or not you wanted to take that long, cold walk in the dark. But, in the end, we always made the trip because, well, when you've got to go, you've got to go.

Given the circumstances of those years, our family home was actually quite comfortable. We lived pretty well compared to a lot of other families in the area. Many poor farmers in our community would have counted themselves lucky to be in our shoes. The boxcar even had heat in the form of a wood-burning stove (I'm told that as a baby I was sometimes put to sleep in its warm oven compartment when I was ailing). And at Christmas time, my grandmother Lois would decorate both the inside and outside of the boxcars with homemade ornaments.

My grandmother Lois stood just under 5 feet tall, yet she was a mighty force. An amazingly hard-working and creative lady, she was a world-class cook (who would routinely do amazing things with a jar of bacon drippings) and housekeeper, making certain the makeshift home was always spotlessly clean, warm and welcoming. People often ask what I liked to eat back then and I answer whatever is set out and I'm the same way today; all food was special to the hungry and I loved more than anything sitting around the table with family. I can also say I remember the joy of boiled beans(lima, butter, Blackeyed-peas, pinto, red and the sweetness of great northern) laced with onions, pork fat, or pig tails and served over stovetop cornbread. Almost every weekend meal was followed up with fried fruit pies and banana cake. Working non-stop for 12-14 hours a day, caring for a dozen of us, my grandmother never voiced a complaint or uttered a coarse word. She and Grandpa Lonnie were achievers and dreamers, yet they were also folks with an innate ability to manage and elevate their environment, whatever it might be, and make the very best of things.

Apparently, not everyone thought that living in a pair of boxcars was an ideal circumstance, but I recall my grandmother telling me, "Whatever you see as a home for someone – even if others are critical or laughing – that home is their home and 'a step up for somebody.'" And so our attitude was that even though some people might stare at our home with amusement or even disdain, we were still better off than many. Though we never stopped dreaming of better times, everyone seemed grateful and proud of what we had.

* * *

Even in tiny Illmo, Missouri, though, larger events had a way of catching up with us. When the United States entered World War II, my father shipped out to the Pacific, where his duties as a Navy cook expanded to encompass just about anything that needed getting done and that was considered doable by an enlisted man of color. We had seen little of my father in the early years of my life. But now, of course, we saw him not at all. Yet that didn't change our day-to-day existence as much as another event: Every spring for several years, the Illmo area experienced massive river flooding. This complicated both Grandpa Lonnie's railway work and Grandma Lois's housekeeping process.

My paternal grandfather, Sylvester Jackson, despairing the constant flooding situation in Illmo, arrived one day and simply packed up the entire household. He placed everyone in the back of a truck with all our worldly possessions and moved us – now 14 in total – to Edwardsville, Illinois, 15 miles across the river from St. Louis. Edwardsville, a small town of 4,800, was the county seat of Madison County. It had some historical significance as a place where Abraham Lincoln both practiced law and, later, gave a speech on the courthouse steps. Ironically, the ideals Lincoln expounded were soon to be put to the test right there. I was 4 or 5 when we arrived in Edwardsville, and unbeknownst to me, while I was in my formative years, I was about to experience the rewards and the painful sutures of social integration in *its* formative years.

What I saw when I got to our Edwardsville home looked liked a castle to me. It was the biggest, highest house on a hill; the locals called it "Nigger Hill." Grandpa Sylvester had built the two-story, six-room dwelling himself. Sylvester was a brilliant, innovative guy who I have always thought of as an electrical engineer minus the college degree. In retrospect, it was no surprise that he managed to construct a house that was well-appointed and large enough to comfortably accommodate the entire sprawling Jackson-White family. He had a way with money and a way with people, both Black and White. He was both streetwise and sophisticated, a charismatic man who somehow always managed to wheel and deal until he got exactly what he needed. As it turns out, I had two exceptional role models in my grandfathers. And if the industrious Lonnie and the ingenious Sylvester didn't always see eye to eye, I can vouch for the fact that they always respected one another, and always looked out for me and for the rest of our brood.

We took up residence in that house on the hill with immense enthusiasm. Since I was the only boy without a brother, I slept with my four uncles – three at the head of the bed and me and Uncle Bob across the bottom. Uncle Bob, my mother's youngest brother, was actually 18 months younger than I, but since he was technically my uncle I called him "Old Bob." The conversations held by our elder uncles – Eugene, Lonnie and Morris – offered "Old Bob" and me a life-changing curriculum on work, financial management, travel, race relations and women (the latter mostly thanks to Uncle Lonnie, a true ladies' man who later in life confided in me that he fathered 32 children – that he knew of!). Those guys would argue, laugh, tell stories and debate every issue imaginable until the early hours of the morning. "Old Bob" and I never complained about the talking; we only lamented our inability to remain awake for all of the stories because of school the next day.

Our Edwardsville house stood directly across Highway 66 from the beautiful all-white public high school. We would watch white students cross the campus to that palace of learning as we walked to the Blacks-only Lincoln School many blocks across town. The Lincoln School had only four teachers, but one of them was extremely special to me. She was my step-grandmother, Alma Aitch-Jackson. Grandpa Sylvester had lost his first wife, my grandmother Marjorie (the 6-foot-2, 250-pound love of his life) during child birth when she was 31. As a widower and a successful man, he found himself quite the desirable "catch," and wound up marrying the local schoolteacher – whose social status in the Black community at that time was roughly equivalent to that of a queen. As far as I was concerned, Miss Alma Aitch was genuine royalty. As tireless as she was talented, she ran her classroom like the tightest of ships.

Actually, I use the term "her classroom" loosely. At the Lincoln School, students in the first through twelfth grade sat in four rooms, and rotated rooms by subject and ability rather than by age. Miss Aitch taught the first, second, third and fourth grades in her room and, let me tell you, you didn't move out of that room until she deemed you good and ready. A 6- or 7-year-old might move up, but a 9- or 10-year-old might still be there. Today, when I go back to the area – in 2007, I purchased the land and the building that housed the old Lincoln School on North Main Street and have so far preserved it as a future site of commercial, academic, or humanitarian significance – I still meet people who will say they were "in my room" as classmates but who might have been five to seven years older than I was.

Between Miss Aitch and Lincoln School's first-rate principal, C.C. (Christopher Columbus) Jones, I believe the amount of dedication and sheer brilliance in that little building was probably greater than that of the rest of the Edwardsville school system put together. Miss Aitch and Mr. Jones fought for us, even when the rest of the city wanted to forget about us or push us aside. They spent quality out-of-school time with kids like me as a matter of course. They were eager to help every child learn because they were dedicated educators who believed the existing social-economic gap was best erased by enlightenment. In those days none of us really knew what was around the corner; if you were Black you had no say and you were the last to know, but the efforts of those teachers would ultimately bring segregated Black children up to par with the white students we would be joining later in integrated junior high and high school classrooms.

Lincoln School was an amazing place with many brilliant students. Richard Penelton, Harry Shaw, the Jason Family, Aunt Dee, the Jones Family, the Brooks Family, and the Hornsberger Family comprised a collection of future Ph.D.s, lawyers, military officers and academic standouts. As a student I had a couple of personal advantages. One is that I got to spend even more time than most with Miss Aitch. It was because of her that I started school as early as I did. My mother continued to work as a domestic when we moved to Edwardsville, and my grandmother often served as my daytime nanny. As school began that fall, when I was 4 years and 5 months old, Miss Aitch decided I had enough going on upstairs to accompany her.

The other advantage I had actually grew out of my mother's work. When I wasn't with Miss Aitch, I would tag along with my mom as she cleaned the houses of well-to-do white families. This was actually a very positive experience for me, because it gave me an idea of what was possible. It was eye-opening to see houses that had lighted rooms, modulated temperatures, not to mention indoor bathrooms. But mostly it was great to be around so many books. To keep myself occupied, I would browse through the collections. We did not have very many books at the Lincoln School, so for me to have a chance to explore them was magical. In the hours my mother worked, I never had time to read an entire book cover to cover, but from a young age I loved to look at the jackets and the pictures, and I learned to read and actually understand the blurbs about the authors by asking questions over and over again. More than once I wondered out loud why Black people didn't write more books and I never got a good answer.

* * *

Apart from starting school, another change was about to take place in my life. When I was 6 years old, my father came home from the military. It is sad to say, but after years of serving his country he came back with an openly bitter attitude regarding racial discrimination. He had initially joined the Navy not to spend years fighting a war, but to get job training and military income to provide for his young wife and family. He was a bright, skilled person, and after the attack on Pearl Harbor – when it was "all hands on deck" to fight the enemy – he, like everyone else, stepped up and did whatever was necessary. But being a cook was the best official job he could achieve in the segregated Navy.

I had not really known my father at all. When he joined our household in Edwardsville, I saw a bitter and sometimes hostile man working hard at two or three different jobs at any one time, dreaming of better times and talking of a future he felt he'd earned and deserved a shot at. My father seemed to work constantly – at least 14 to 16 hours a day. In this way, he was like his own father, Sylvester – both men of incredible energy who just never seemed to tire. (Dad kept that energy up until the age of 91, and would have made it to 100 if his appetite for food and drink weren't as big as the rest of his appetite for life.)

Dad became a laborer, a bartender, the night manager of the Edwardsville Gun Club and eventually a factory foreman for A.O. Smith, an automotive parts manufacturer. The management job was unusual in a world where there were few white-collar jobs for Blacks, aside from the very rare doctor or lawyer. He would work a job, come home and sleep two hours, get up, and go to another job. In between, he was off to Alton, Illinois and taking college classes in criminology. He always dreamed of being a state trooper, imagining how cool it would be to be part of law enforcement and to have a job that came with a gun and a car. After scoring high on the exams, he never got a call back.

My father also became politically active. He was one of the early outspoken pioneers working to accelerate the school integration process at a time when many in the white community were hoping that nightmare scenario would simply go away. Many claimed that integration wouldn't work and the status quo was near perfect for now. "Separate but equal" policies were not working for Black students in any way, yet segregationists believed in state and community rights – meaning no interference from the outside on how their state's tax dollars should be spent. Fortunately, the Supreme Court directive handed down in Brown vs. Board of Education, combined with state and federal revenue realities, accelerated the attention that school districts paid to integration mandates.

Dad met nightly with like-minded neighbors, and occasionally with white sympathizers. Unfortunately, as a result of his participation in those clandestine activities, Dad's credit was shut off. The handshake credit arrangements he enjoyed as a compliant colored man quickly dissolved and were annulled. He also lost his primary job and the "fly by night" local loan company foreclosed on his $2,000 home construction loan. Dad moved to Chicago after finding work in the post office there, while my mom, my sister Marjorie and I moved from our home in Edwardsville into the public housing projects in nearby Newport-Madison, Illinois. My mother retained her job as a domestic in Edwardsville, though, and each day drove us 20 miles back to school in that community. The better my basketball game got, the more often mom was reminded how important this drive was getting to be and would never want for gasoline or complementary car repairs. The game of basketball was becoming an important part of all our lives.

I was glad to keep on attending school in Edwardsville for lots of reasons, one of which was that I could continue to see my best buddy since first grade, Govoner "Gov" Vaughn. Gov and his family were, early on, not full-time Edwardsville residents; they were what we'd call today migrant factory workers, recruited from the South as seasonal labor for the local radiator heating plant, which eventually became a market and price leader in the post-war commercial building boom. The Vaughns would come up from Mississippi in late September and return in late March or early April to go back to farming. I always envied their trips because I felt they had the perfect arrangement. Every kid in that family was an exceptional student with the kind of values only the greatest parenting can provide. Aside from being excellent role models, the Vaughns were always very social, with a knack for making any family gathering a great time. Taylor Vaughn, Gov's dad, stood 6-foot-5, and his four boys were all over 6-foot-3 and very competitive athletes. While in Edwardsville, the family initially lived in a workers' trailer camp until they built their own home closer to the high school and closer to their dad's part-time duties as the neighborhood barber. Gov may not have been around 12 months a year, but the boyhood times I spent with him are among my happiest memories. I loved his entire family and Mrs. Mary, his mother, made me feel at home and basically "adopted" me. Years later

I learned she kept a scrapbook for Gov and one for me documenting my sports achievements. I cherish it to this day.

Like most kids, Gov, his brothers and I played a lot of sports. But, to be honest, until junior high school neither of us had anything special going on athletically. I enjoyed the games, but I wasn't focused. I was preoccupied with practical domestic life issues, like getting wood and searching the railroad tracks for coal. We worried in those days about getting enough to eat, and finding a little space to be by myself once in a while. Physically, I was kind of tall, frail and a little clumsy. The first sports team I tried out for, I didn't make the final roster. I was that kid who always wanted to be with the oldest and best players, but would stand at the back of the group when they were choosing sides during recess. I wasn't at all bothered when I'd overhear someone saying, "I don't want that skinny dude." Those remarks only made me more determined.

Then, once again, there came a big shift in my life. My world began to change in my 12th year the first time I saw the Harlem Globetrotters in St. Louis and heard the Brother Bones whistling rendition of the song "Sweet Georgia Brown." The smooth, skillful feats the Globetrotter players performed on the basketball court and the jubilant reaction of the crowds truly amazed me. I'd never before seen Black men so strong, so cool, or so respected by everyone present: Black folks, White folks, young and old.

I was so moved that, incredibly, I walked right up to Abe Saperstein, the man who had founded the team in Chicago, Illinois, in 1927 (24 years earlier) and said, "I want to be here. How do you get here?" He shook my hand and said just the right thing: He would look forward to that day after I finished college. I remember thinking, "What the heck does college have to do with it?" But the seed was planted. I'm sure

Abe told a million little kids like me the same thing, but for me it stuck.

A few months later, when the 1951 *Harlem Globetrotters* movie came out, I camped out in Edwardsville's Wildy Theater on the corner of Main Street and Hillsboro – upstairs balcony on the right – six rows reserved for Blacks only. I saw that movie at least 10 times. It was the first time I had seen Black people as sports heroes and in a film where they weren't dancing or Uncle Tom-ing as waiters and porters. I began to dream the story; the only difference was the movie of my dreams had me in it. I was two Trotters superstars, combined: The embodiment of 5-foot-10 dribbling wizard Marques Haynes and 6-foot-7 Bill Townsend, whose speed and shooting style struck a chord.

The double dose of seeing the team and meeting Abe and then seeing that film had a powerful impact. I had hoped there would be more to life than what was around me. I knew there was something greater to aspire to than street ball, getting something good to eat or hanging around with the guys. Now I saw firsthand that there was a life outside the box or, more accurately, outside the boxcar. I was beginning to see the way to respect and its rewards.

I believe that everything became possible because of the fire my dreams ignited inside me. I feel sad that today so many kids, Black and White, appear to have simply stopped dreaming. To me, as long as one is fed and has a roof over their head, poverty is about the absence of visions and dreams, even though one's day-to-day existence may be tolerable. Our job as parents and leaders is to give the next generation a reason to dream. When someone has dreams and hopes, regardless of income, they begin to ascend psychologically to the mythical social/economic place of life referred to as middle class (a holding place of hope). Middle class is a relative term and not always about real money in absolute terms; it is a matter of a sense of imagined security and a place to dream and hope for respect and better tomorrows. To my mind, one is middle class as long as you believe there is somewhere for you to go with your dreams and your life purpose is focused on that place – whether that destination is college or a next rung on the job ladder, or something else respectful and meaningful that you envision in your pursuit of happiness. At age 60 I came to a realization that dreams and life are more about the journey than the destination. I wish I'd focused on this sooner; because once I did, for me life and career achievements as well as the creation of wealth became significantly simpler and more meaningful.

Sometimes I fear living in dismal transformational times without strong transformational leaders because it causes society to get near a tipping point where more and more people simply visualize quitting the journey. I wish it weren't so; I fear this kind of negative collectivism and in my way I will keep doing what I can to reverse this trend by helping develop future leaders.

I was blessed to have been raised in a big family of leaders, hard workers and big dreamers. I know that for me a dream was the beginning, but it's also important to say it was not the end. It's true what they say about success being part inspiration and a bigger part perspiration. After seeing the Globetrotters, I became so attached to my basketball it was like a new appendage. While working at LeClaire Park in Edwardsville, sweeping off the basketball courts, I discovered that I could run faster and jump higher than anyone my age. That summer, I actually dunked a tennis ball and, later, a basketball. I was 13 at the time and already 5-foot-10, so my skill got noticed. It feels strange to be remembering junior high school and high school and even weirder to be actually writing about it; but I find like most people it's the only way we can make some sense out of where we've gotten to, so bare with me on all this as I attempt to paint this picture for you because it's the only way I've learned to make any sense of how a person living on dirt at the very bottom of society starts to believe they are special, with a destiny of wealth and leadership. I was actually starting to believe at age twelve I was someone special, with gifts in leadership and intuition. Imagine waking up everyday feeling the opposite; and no one cares or pays attention. I don't doubt for one moment that basketball is fun but in the real scheme of life its often overrated and can be a little stupid. All I can say is, if you don't get it, find your own hook or game. It was becoming clear to me that if I put the same effort and time into other areas and phases of my life that I had put into basketball, anything was possible – and my dreams would still turn likely to reality.

2 WHATEVER IT TAKES

"Are you ever going to stop dribbling that damn ball?"

My mother just about threatened to have me committed. Day and night, rain and shine, I was shooting, running, jumping and dribbling.

Was I ever going to stop dribbling that damn ball? *"No, ma'am."*

Once I contracted basketball fever, or the "basketball Jones" as some say, I made the all-important mental connection of work and preparation as a formula for success as I never had before. It might sound obvious in retrospect, but to me it was an epiphany: There is a cause-and-effect relationship between preparation, hard work, success and reward. The magic of making a commitment and practicing, practicing, practicing turned on like a light bulb in my insecure and sometimes foolish adolescent head, and for the first time I could visualize the first and most important steps of connecting dreams to reality.

Up until this time, I thought the secret of life, if there was such a thing, was, "Let time pass, let nature take its course by doing just enough to stay hidden, keep out of harm's way, and get by." Whether in sports or at school or mowing the lawn, I had a lot of dreams, but I had no goal – unless you consider just skating along to be a goal itself. (I did this very expertly.)

It took many years to understand why sports motivated me to work so hard and why schoolwork was a distant second. I knew school wasn't difficult at all, but no one ever gave me one good reason for studying. I can remember deciding to really study for a high school final exam and I scored a 98. Except for Gov's brother Taylor Vaughn saying "good work," no one else said a thing. I recall thinking: *That was easy but not all that satisfying.* I knew I could do it, but there was no need to waste my time. Yet what the game meant to my dreams was accolades and immediate approval from friends, family and white folks. Where were my Jackie Robinson or Globetrotters of science? Why didn't Goose Tatum tell me he owed that deadly hook shot to the study of math?

I knew intuitively then, as I do now, that humans need hope and visible reasons to set directions and excel. I saw my parents and grandparents' unimpeachable work ethic, yet we were on the low end of the economic ladder. Outside our small neighborhood I felt fear and witnessed blind subservience to the power structure, but I hadn't realized that I too was internalizing all this and losing hope. It's been said many times that democracy and capitalism are built on foundations of trust and, most importantly, hope. For example, meaningful work, achieving middle class upward mobility, and helping others are all reasons to live and reasons for hope. Like a lot of young people, I hadn't felt any hope, and my significant goals had been rare. I certainly wasn't into the notion of expending a lot of unnecessary energy for the inevitable and expected marginal results from a segregated society. I was looking for a drug or instant fix and mine would come from the accolades received from sports.

I'll never forget young Emmett Till and the times prior to his murder (the 14-year-old boy would be beaten, lynched and drowned in Money, Mississippi in 1955 after reportedly flirting with a white woman). I heard about segregation, racism, and the importance of conducting yourself; I knew and disliked the drills as I was constantly being warned and reminded day in and day out. The threats to my psyche were incessant and seemingly came from every direction, feeding the majority of my internal childhood fears. I realized that, slowly but surely, racism and the fear it caused within my being were conspiring to define my life and to create the improbability of fulfilling any ambition or dreams I might ever have.

As I've gotten older I often hear people say that the moment of definition and vulnerability in their life was the personal impact of, perhaps, the 1962 Cuban missile crisis, the stock market collapse in 1929, the bombing of Pearl Harbor in 1941, the 9/11 World Trade Center bombings in 2001, the Martin Luther King or John F. Kennedy assassinations. For me, it's what happened to young Emmett Till on that day of August 21, 1955. But that would come later...

In the summer of 1952, when I was between sixth and seventh grades, I still had innocence. I found my reason for hope when I discovered not books, but the magic of basketball. My motto evolved to *whatever it takes in life to achieve a goal*. I was now on a mission to master a game. In the future, this mission was to bring me confidence, hundreds of wonderful friendships and experiences, and millions of dollars – because the game also taught me to trust, to lead, to prepare, to listen and to work. But as of now I had simply found happiness; my reason outside our now sprawling family to live and believe. Inside the very core of basketball there was no prejudice; you either could play or not play and teams that wanted to win were color blind. More importantly, teams with the best players that worked hard and smart were never denied. That was the rule of my new playground. I discovered I had a level of skill and the opportunity to win, and I was willing to work and sweat and sweat and work until I actually earned the prizes of respect and recognition that would separate me from all the others in my family and give me some family status. I dreamed of one day achieving the greatness I saw in my grandparents, my mother and my dad, and I dreamed, mostly and always, of getting better and better.

* * *

I was first dubbed "Shooter" in a Lincoln Junior High basketball game. Our team had been bussed to East St. Louis to play against other Black middle schoolers. East St. Louis was a harsh ghetto town, famous for weekend shootings and fights that usually had nothing to do with basketball. We were playing in front of a raucous gathering of drop-ins and relatives of the opposing team. This was a tough, cool, street-smart town where people didn't need a reason to fight. Nevertheless, it seems that I, a basically non-basketball-playing seventh grader, would unwittingly give them a reason.

At that time I felt, without a doubt, like the most underrated player on our team. Out of 10 guys, you could say I was number 11: a real benchwarmer. But because we were losing badly that day – by a score of 66 to 15 – my coach figured what the hell, he had nothing to lose by putting me in at the very end of the game. I borrowed a friend's gym shoes and with seconds to go I went in and made an improbable shot. Just as the buzzer went off I had upped our score from 15 to 17. Obviously we still lost, but it turned out that my last-minute shot had apparently tipped some spectator bets that had to do with the point spread or the over and under – who knows. I guess a few people had heard of our pitiful team and thought, "These guys are never going to score more than 15 points." Now some money that had already changed hands had to be handed back. This made some onlookers very unhappy. And in typical East St. Louis fashion, they started a brawl that became a free-for-all, which spilled onto the court, and took on a kind of life of its own.

Our coach yelled in panic, "Get your stuff. Let's get outta here!" We all high-tailed it to the bus. Though the crowd rushed the bus and started banging on the windows, we managed to make it out of town unharmed. Everyone was scared and shaking until we got a couple of miles down the road. When we finally felt like we could breathe again, the coach looked at me and yelled, "Shooter, how the hell would *you* of all people shoot that ball?" Then everyone, including me, broke out laughing in unison – though in truth, I was pretty mortified.

Later, when my athletic accomplishments became media events, most of my childhood friends were somewhat shocked, but some were not totally surprised. They had seen my work habits, desire and commitment grow until I was, after all, deserving of the moniker "Shooter." But that ironic name slowly faded as my skills became legitimate.

* * *

The next year, as I was to enter the eighth grade, the Edwardsville schools integrated. My new school, the Columbus School, had nice indoor and outdoor courts with nets and several regulation balls. Word had already spread in the community about the skill of some of the new Black basketball players, and right away – before we even left the Lincoln School – the teachers started to watch as some of us played on our little outdoor schoolyard court during recess. It wasn't long before one of the teachers told the Columbus basketball coach, Coach Gregor, who checked out us Lincoln School transfers and immediately invited us for tryouts. Soon Gov and I, along with Sam Johnson, were to become official members of the Columbus Junior High Wildcats.

Very quickly, I went from being a substitute to being very good for my age and the team's top scorer. Through the magic of practice and repetition, I discovered that I could shoot a basketball in this weird-looking Globetrotters manner that no one had seen before. I would jump really high, arch my back, hold the ball in back of my head with two hands and I'd just flip it or let it fly right over the arms of whoever was defending me. I favored this shot because I was a high jumper, and also because having my arms and shoulders behind my head gave me the extra strength and leverage I needed to just flick the ball upward to the basket from any distance. This kind of "fade away" shooting style is a lot more common nowadays, but for a while my name was almost synonymous with the fade-away flick shot. Back in those Columbus Wildcat games, the defense started to double-team me, with one man in front and one behind. Still, I racked up the points. As eighth graders, we never lost and became the talk of the southern part of the state. Illinois and Indiana took their small-town basketball very seriously – almost fanatically; it was the only thing most people in those sometimes dusty farm towns could agree on in those times.

* * *

By the time I got to Edwardsville High School, I was beginning to expand my world view. For a couple of summers, when I wasn't in school, I had been working for a golf professional named Howie Popham at a local country club. Howie was a good man and after a couple of years of watching me caddy, shine shoes, clean tables and wash dishes, he tried to convince me I would be foolish to sacrifice the $30 cash a week I was averaging from those chores in exchange for more education. I loved the exhilaration of having a job and the money and the independence it brought, and Howie made his case very convincingly. He'd say, "You have a dream job now. Who do you know in the 'colored' community that's doing better?"

I thought to myself, "Howie just may be right – but *is this it*?" I decided it wasn't. And for me, this conversation became yet another internal call to action. I was going to do big things, I was going to help my family, and I was never, never going to look back at my friend Howard Popham. I wanted to be great, be respected like my grandfather, have money, and be able to give back to neighbors in need the way my father and grandfather were doing.

I joined the Edwardsville High basketball team along with Bill Penelton, Gov, and Gov's cousin, Jim Vaughn. A year later, Bob White – "Old Uncle Bob" – would join as well. Our white teammates included Kenneth "Buzz" Shaw, who retired as president of Syracuse University, and Harold Patton, later an internationally recognized patent attorney for Medtronic Corporation in Minneapolis. Four of the starting five became Division I players, graduated college, and have remained friends to this day. All of us played under the watchful eye of a very smart and tough Italian coach named Joe Lucco.

Coach Lucco stood ramrod straight, slicked his Black hair straight back from his forehead, and dressed like he just stepped out of *GQ*. His impeccable suits fit like they were tailor-made, his collars were well-pressed, his ties perfectly matched. (He was, in fact, the man who taught me how to tie a necktie.) He had the most beautiful watches I ever saw. He stood all of 5 feet, 5 inches, yet he looked like a man who was ready to win – the proverbial little big man.

Lucco would eventually become the single most unforgettable inspiration in my life. He was the quintessential leader and an excellent teacher of the game. If race was ever a problem for him, he disguised it well. Coach never gave me any slack, but I knew he cared deeply for me. He would always say he demanded more because he knew I had more to give.

I have to admit, while I never said a lot, there were times I would act like quite the swaggering hot shot "jock." But Coach Lucco had a way of dealing with that. For instance, I eventually lived across the street from the high school in a house we shared with my grandparents (my mom and sister still lived in the housing project, but I had to be near school because of all the practice). Living so close I developed the habit, on days of travel games, of waiting until the team's bus or cars pulled up to the school and watching everyone else board before I sauntered across Route 66 which at the time ran right through the center of Edwardsville. One day, the day of a big game with our rival Wood River, 10 or 15 miles away, Coach Lucco apparently got tired of waiting on my Hollywood act and said, "If Mannie Jackson's not here on time, we are not waiting." To everyone's horror – including my own – he told the driver to head out. (His son Billy revealed to me and to others years later that Joe was frightened but wouldn't back down. He had to set an example.)

I remember thinking, "Damn, they *left* me." I panicked and called one of my uncles who told me he would send his friend, a taxi driver, over to take me to Wood River. I arrived five minutes before the game and $10 lighter in my wallet. My teammates were happy to see me, but Coach Lucco only asked, "Did you come to play?" Then he took me aside and told me he would reimburse me for cab fare if I scored 20 points. That sounded OK to me. The only thing was, as a disciplinary measure, Coach didn't plan to start me. It was only toward the end of the first half that he finally put me in. I had honestly never been nervous in a game before, but now I was. Fortunately I ended up scoring 24 points.

The story that came out of that day has been told many, many times over the years to young people in Edwardsville and beyond. It became like an Aesop's fable, the moral of which was: Be on time! *If they can leave without Mannie Jackson*, parents would tell their sons and daughters, *they can leave without anyone.*

Another result of that episode was that people always asked me, "Did Lucco give you the $10?" My answer was always the same: He gave me that and so much more, for the rest of my life.

I said Coach Lucco was an amazing leader. That's an easy thing to say about someone in general, but let me break down exactly what I mean. What made him someone who commanded such loyalty and admiration?

For one thing, he was one of the best communicators I ever met. Whether he was giving a speech to hundreds of people – which as the years went on, he did frequently – or simply talking to the team in a locker room, he was transfixing. He had a way of emoting and of punctuating his points that made you pay attention and remember what he said.

Next, for all his flamboyance, he paid supreme attention to the minutest detail and was always prepared. He was more prepared than anyone I ever met since, even in the world of big business. After each game, win or lose, he would be awake until midnight, reviewing. Before each game, he was in at 5:00 or 6:00 a.m., planning how we would score against our opponents. Because of his example, I became even more dedicated to the game. For example, when Uncle Bob joined the team, Coach Lucco knew that Bob and I would stay in the gym two hours after every home game to practice and replay every shot. (The night janitor paid us a dollar and trusted us to turn out the lights and clean the locker room.)

Finally, Lucco understood our dreams and supported them. He was a courageous man who instilled courage in us. Often we needed that courage. We had many challenges other than outscoring our competitors during those years. In the mid-50s in southern Illinois, where a recently integrated small school was creating an unlikely athletic legend, acceptance and racial equality off the playing field had its limits.

During away tournaments that involved overnight stays, we were offered lodging with families of color because hotels wouldn't always accept us. Even on our own team, towels were once dyed black and orange – one stack for myself, Gov, Bob and Jim Vaughn, and one for white teammates. Coach Lucco would only say, "Focus on the big stuff. One day you and Gov will own this town and this school. Let's you and me get there together." And he'd add in a kind and sly way, "By the way, Shooter, take any towel you want. This is your team." I learned to focus on the right things, and eventually we made black towels an important symbol of our strength, not our weakness.

On road trips, we couldn't eat in most restaurants with our white teammates. Unfortunately, this was true even in some spots in our hometown. Imagine today: a player averaging nearly 30 points a game, being Basketball Player of the Year for the state, and eating in a kitchen across the street from his high school while all the fans, media, students and white teammates look on from the main dining room.

A former Chicago Bear and National Football League Hall of Famer was the county sheriff at the time and father of a girl named Toni, one of Gov's and my best friends and the team's star cheerleader. The good-natured sheriff owned the biggest and most popular downtown restaurant (where, as a young boy I had once worked shining shoes) and after returning from away games everyone on the team went there to celebrate an out-of-town victory. The restaurant had a strict "no-Blacks-served" policy, no matter what the circumstances. So after a night when Gov and I had led the team to another win, we joined our relatives who were working in the kitchen and had a great meal, compliments of the employees. I remember looking out through the small opening where they served the food and seeing our teammates, their girlfriends and their families. Some might come up and say, "Nice game Mannie, Gov," and we would speak to them through that small hole in the wall.

The same no-Blacks-served practice existed at Idlewood Inn, a small restaurant/hangout across the street from the school. We weren't allowed to leave the kitchen in this little eating place and sit with our teammates, and to my knowledge no one voiced an opinion that this too was hypocritical or stupid.

My sister called me to her home recently and asked me to look over my graduating class yearbook; she said "I want to show you why I worried about you so much in those days and another reason why what you accomplished is so unbelievable." In a couple seconds, I realized except for a very few class photos, Blacks were completely invisible – as in not seen or mentioned in that commemorative document. There were no people of color as teachers and in the award and recognition section the photos were all white; including best athlete, prom king and queen, most likely to succeed, etc. Every one of the 15 or so clubs were mostly all white, as were their leaders. On Page 56, the annual stage production BLACK FACE, which drew enthusiastic white audiences, BLACK FACE- quartet a la minstrel was proudly displayed. Black students were offended by this production and a few Black and White students voiced disapproval and we were dismissed, as if the weight of our objection did not matter, because we did not appreciate the show as "art."

In 2011, by which time we were all senior citizens, I talked to several teammates about this incident and told them that to this day I have a social scar from those times and it still bothers me. A couple responded they, too, felt badly; some said they weren't aware it bothered us. Then I asked my most troubling question: Did they do nothing because that's just the way it was or, deep inside, did they ever feel that's the way it was supposed to be? Would they stand up today to protect or protest injustice or silly prejudices? First, the room went quiet. Then almost everyone in the room spoke freely and openly about the events of that time and their personal contributions to progress in eradicating intolerance. Most would say it was because of Herman Shaw, Bill or Harry Penelton, the Vaughn brothers and sisters, and others from the Hill, Lower Town or the all Black trailer camp that they came to realizations of human rights. For a moment, I was allowed to feel really good about my little and once bigoted hometown, and all was forgiven.

Because of Lucco and the quality of the guys in our group, we never had a single racial incident within the team – although some parents complained about our taking roster spots and playing time away from "regular (white) kids." Those concerns soon went away and the new roster was just accepted as part of the 1950s' new way of life. After all, wasn't being the best we could be more important than the team's color scheme? My role models in those days were Jackie Robinson, Joe Louis and Goose Tatum. (As Jesse Jackson once said, "We are all proud to say America's sports industry generates billions of dollars of revenue and thousands of jobs. We may not have ever known how great it could become without desegregation.") My hat's off to the Harlem Globetrotters for whipping the crap out of the World Champion Lakers a couple years in a row; because prior to that, all I heard was Black kids weren't smart enough to play organized ball alongside whites.

During high school games, we heard every racial epithet imaginable shouted from the crowds: nigger, jungle bunny, and the like. Of course we were fully able to fight, but we didn't; we loved our coaches and teammates and didn't want to jeopardize our growing stature as a team. No matter what, Gov and I would calmly go about the business of winning games and embarrassing our opponents. Under the guidance of Lucco, we quickly learned that the most powerful weapon in our arsenal was our talent and we set about to show our skill without showing emotion. To this day, I don't know if that approach was right or wrong, but it worked for us.

Many years later, someone sent me films they had taken of some of our state championship tournament games. I noticed then to what extremes we had taken our deliberately unemotional demeanor. I saw that whatever was going on around us or on the court, Gov and I never talked to one another, never smiled, never grimaced, never high-fived. I had the impression we were like robots, or maybe functioning under some sort of "stay out of trouble, stay focused" hypnotic spell.

This automaton-like demeanor seemed especially interesting to me in light of the fact that Gov and I always had our own crazy, laugh-out-loud little games going on within almost every game. We would strive to get far enough ahead and then give the audience something to remember and talk about. (I had reached the point where I had stopped getting stronger as an all around player and became focused on being a scoring machine.) Along with this, a gentleman named Spike Riley would give me 50 cents if I dunked the first score of the game. This kind of lively fun should have given us something to smile about. Maybe we had to anesthetize ourselves to everything and everybody out of necessity. The blinders we had to put on to block out the racial comments blocked everything else out at once. To this day I don't remember or recall the so-called "good old days" of high school or college for that matter, because many of the non-basketball experiences in both instances were wildly surreal and hurtful.

After the games, Gov and I would often go out and have a great time. Late into the night we would eat barbecued ribs and fried catfish, drink orange soda water, and listen to the Five Satins, the Heartbeats, Johnny Ace, Ike and Tina, the Dells, Sam Cooke, the Chantels, B. B. King and the best blues artists in the country. I've never talked to Gov about this, but we felt the hurt then, although we didn't allow our egos or sensitivities to get involved or to process anything while we played. We simply hadn't learned to hate or allow the Black-White situation to break through our shield with words and disrupt what we had going on and the many changes we were making every day. Besides that, we were in the company of a lot of very classy and good people. Somehow we just always knew this.

In a way, despite everything going on around me, I created and dwelt in my own emotional cocoon. I dreamed endlessly of being the best and reaching the top, but no one bothered to caution me about the roadblocks or discuss the scale and the impersonal reality of racism.

From 1955 on, I'd have Emmett Till flashbacks and quickly shake them off. I was just so drugged by success and sports adoration that I didn't listen or see the reality of many racial events around me clearly or closely enough.

While in high school I had one hard-to-shake overriding temptation and that was to transfer to Indianapolis, Indiana. My uncle was a chiropractor there and a big fan of Crispus Attucks High School, a national basketball power. He'd brag and tell his friends I was a better player than Oscar Robertson. When he'd come home he'd say, "Leave this prejudice country shit behind and come to a city and live with me and your aunt." It was tempting because I was haunted by the desire to play with or against the "Big 0." Often when I'd hear booing and obscene language at games, I'd think *I'm getting out of here*. But as the noise turned to applause and words of encouragement, I'd look over at Lucco and Gov and think, *what could be better?* Little white kids would wait for us after games just to touch us. Media from all over the country photographed our every move. The most beautiful young girls from the opposing team schools, Black and White, summoned the nerve to approach us.

We knew better, of course, than to make a habit of going off "sneakin" with white girls. No matter how much we may have been tempted, we understood that to be caught meeting a white girl out on the countryside or riding around in cars with them might easily end with us wrecking someone's life, getting beat up – or, far worse, getting "Emmett Tilled." We may have tried it a few times, but never got addicted to "sneakin," to the night life, or to booze. Against the odds, I did develop a strong platonic friendship with a white girl during those years. Her name was Margo Kriege. She became a high-powered European bank executive and a renowned monetary policy expert, and our friendship endured and grew as we watched the world around us evolve. In college she would proudly introduce me to her boyfriends and friends as her best friend, and she would check on me constantly if I were ever sick or hurt. She knew all about my fears and insecurities. She was beautiful, with oversized eyes, a big face, big smile, and boundless energy. Later in life Margo would push me to co-author a book with her. At her funeral service a few years ago, I had the honor of saying a few words in remembrance and met members of her new family. I am sure at least one of them called me Uncle Mannie.

Gov and I always knew that he and I had each other's backs and that hundreds of others, Black and White, would literally give their lives for us. As a result of Coach Joe Lucco's basketball success, he was in great demand as a post-season banquet speaker and would take me along for the two- to three-hour drives and we'd talk about things in life other than basketball. He would sometimes look over at his son Billy (now a prominent attorney) and tell audiences that I was like another son to him. One almost could see racial attitudes shifting on those evenings. Lucco was a powerful and excellent speaker who inspired audiences with his stories, value system and accomplishments – not the least of which was his competitive advantage of being able to motivate and develop the Black student-athlete. He would conclude his talks by saying, "I'm good at what I do because I love what I do, and I've learned to chase my dreams and will always *believe*." After a pause, often accompanied by a standing ovation, he would look over at me and simply say in a muted tone not always heard by everyone, "Not bad for a first-generation Italian. We won again." We'd exit the building like rock stars and start the drive home. (Coach Lucco later became superintendent of schools and concluded his career as an Illinois state senator. To this day I feel Billy Lucco and his sister Marina are extended family.)

* * *

My own family was proud and supportive during my high school years. My sister Marjorie was special; she was a social magnate and stuck by me no matter what, never missing a game or event. She knew the game as an expert and didn't miss a play. She was my number one fan and would follow her big brother to the ends of the earth. She, Nina Beard, our town's city clerk and Paul Smith were always on hand then and today for any Mannie Jackson event. Ironically, some of the family, for all their support, couldn't quite understand what all the fuss was about. Grandpa Sylvester had such a limited understanding of basketball *per se* that he once left a game at halftime, thinking, "Well, they stopped running around. It must be over. He'd say to me, "It's alright to do sports if you don't let it get in the way of important things."

What important things? To me, at that point, life was still all about basketball. School, for the most part, was something that filled in the time between games. Yes, I had some very caring teachers. Two of them, Ms. Barbara Moomaw and Ms. Joan Edwards, apparently saw something in me and took me into their homes and their hearts, spending hours bringing me up to speed in the areas where I had some catching up to do. (I had never been taught what a "noun" or a "preposition" was, which caused quite a few snickers among classmates.)

And, yes, I still retained my passion for books that had begun when I obsessively leafed through the volumes I found in the houses my mother cleaned. When I was asked to write my first book report in eighth grade, on *Snowbound* by John Greenleaf Whittier, I read that small book over and over until I could have recited it backwards and forwards.

But for all my love of reading and, ultimately, writing and science, academics were decidedly on a back burner for me. Sadly, some Black classmates – who were naturally smart on and off the court, yet struggled with class work – never recovered from the scholastic opportunity lost during the years that preceded integration. I found I could get B grades in the right classes without thinking too much about it, and that was fine by me. I knew I would go to a good college, and that academics would certainly not stand in the way, but I also knew I was not going via the usual route.

Our last two years at Edwardsville, we advanced to the quarterfinals and finals of the Sweet 16, which is the Illinois state high school tournament. This included all schools in the state, since Illinois was not broken down by classification, even though our little school had fewer than 800 students. My drive and desire, my commitment to doing *whatever it takes*, had paid off. I scored just under 30 points per game in the regular season and was selected All-State in my junior and senior years and Illinois Player of the Year as a senior.

At 6-foot-2, I had a 44-inch vertical leap that enabled me to sail over nearly anyone in my way. Gov, who was 6-foot-4, was already the greatest clutch shooter I would ever see. The two of us were not surprised when colleges came calling, though even we – confident and cocky as we were in our star status – were unprepared for the level at which we were to be courted to play the big-time college game. Made no sense to me then and it doesn't today.

3 AN EDUCATION

Wilt Chamberlain was on the phone. For me!

The man had already become a legend playing for the Kansas University Jayhawks; his skill, speed and endurance were unparalleled in the NCAA. Now Jayhawks coach Dick Harp had asked Wilt to intervene on his behalf. Rumor had it I was leaning toward some other schools – Seton Hall, Marquette, the University of Illinois – and the rumor was right. I greatly liked and respected Wilt, whom I had met before, and it was incredibly cool that he was asking me to be his teammate, but I was a senior at Edwardsville by then and it had taken me quite a while to narrow down my choices. The very rural Lawrence, Kansas was definitely not among them.

Early in my high school career, I slowly began learning about the college scholarship process. Former Edwardsville athletes would return and tell us they were attending one school or another and that the institution paid for their expenses and gave them cars, clothes and cash. I found all this to be amazing, but Gov and I wondered whether there was a factor that might take us out of the running. We felt we were as talented, or more, than many of those guys, but they were also white.

Coach Lucco was always encouraging. He repeated a mantra: "Stay out of trouble, stay away from white girls, stay committed in the classroom and you'll receive the big scholarships." He turned out to be right – although that part about white girls, whose advances we were still dodging, seemed especially unfair in light of the fact that there were only three or four Black girls in our graduating class.

By my junior year, college recruiters were contacting me, and by the following winter the pressure was intense. Some schools backed away when they learned I was Black, but I still received over 100 serious inquiries and offers. As for "what was in it for me," I heard it all.

The things it was legal for Division I schools to offer student athletes were – back then as well as today – room, board, tuition, payment for books and a job. But in reality an offer from a team in the Big Ten or other conference might include a car, clothes, money and a good job for my father. Some of the offers were extraordinary. One school in the mountain region offered $40,000 by putting $10,000 into an account for each of my four college years. That was a boatload of money back then – not too bad a sum even today. This team had managed to recruit a lot of great athletes from urban East and West Coast high schools. I guess it was no secret how they got there.

The truth is, though, that in my experience, 80 to 90 percent of schools "crossed the line" when it came to recruiting. I didn't think of it as right or wrong; it was just the way it was. I thought that most of the offers made to me were appropriate in terms of the marketplace, because I heard very similar offers from more than one school. But I didn't like some of the characters who made the offers. I tended to go with my gut, steering clear of coaches, assistant coaches, scouts or boosters whom I judged to be racist, sleazy or just not the kind of people I wanted to be around.

The NCAA aside, I had one extremely tempting offer in my senior year. I was contacted by Phil Brownstein, a scout for my beloved Harlem Globetrotters. The Globetrotters had recently attracted a lot of media attention by signing a few high school stars, like the great 6-foot-9 point guard J.C. Gibson from Jefferson High School in Los Angeles, and developing them into box office hits.

There was nothing wrong with the Globetrotters taking kids right out of high school. Some of those kids weren't qualified to go to college or had no interest in doing so. But when Abe Saperstein discovered I had been asked to bypass college, he was furious. Abe was a resident of Chicago, a University of Illinois alumnus, and a close friend of Doug Mills, then the athletic director at U of I. He knew the school was after me, and he thought it was a great match. Abe told me again: Go to college, get a degree, and then see him afterward, when there would be a spot for me on my dream team.

In the end, I did choose the University of Illinois. Abe was supportive of that decision, and so was Coach Lucco, but the main reason I went was because Gov had made up his mind. He was going no place else but the University of Illinois, with its Champaign-Urbana campus a mere two hours from home. I wanted the two of us to stay together. In addition to being my on-court soul mate, I knew Gov would have my back off the court.

Gov and I had been through things together I felt no on else would comprehend. For example, on summer weekends we would congregate with others on outdoor basketball courts in Indianapolis, Edwardsville, Alton and East St. Louis for exhibitions that sometimes drew large crowds. After these summer games, we'd hear what a great performance it was: "The best we've ever seen." One night, two carloads of us were driving home from East St. Louis, feeling full of ourselves, and stopped at a dive to get something to drink. Several customers recognized us and asked for autographs. Finally, I approached the bar and ordered Cokes to go. "Get the fuck out of here," said the bartender. He reached under the bar, pulled out a gun, pointed it at my face and said, "I want you out of here now, and tell those other niggers to get out of my parking lot, or I'll blow your heads off." The place got instantly still. We slowly backed out the door, got into the car and drove off. No one said a word about the incident on the drive home, nor have we discussed it since. But the bond created by those experiences is difficult to sever.

Another factor in my decision for Illinois was a former teammate, Don Ohl, who was already at the U of I. Don was an Edwardsville High alumnus; as a sophomore I played with him and learned a lot about moving without the ball and coming off picks. He's the only person I'd ever met that loved to shoot and score as much as I did. Don Ohl was a brilliant, solid player and He and Gov were the best combination of shooters and defenders we had ever had in the state of Illinois. (Ohl later played over 10 seasons in the NBA as an All-Star and by all measures should be a Hall of Famer.) He was also no doubt the coolest white guy I'd ever known. Playing with him was like playing with someone from the streets, his game was so tight. (What's more, playing with him all those years was one of the reasons I knew Gov and I should have had long careers in the NBA.) I loved the idea of a U of I team stacked with three strong players from the same hometown and believed the combination of Gov, Ohl and myself would be unbeatable.

The University of Illinois hadn't made an over-the-top offer but, as was completely usual and customary, they did give me some perks. Apart from my scholarship and school expenses, I had a generous clothing allowance (I could spend $250 at a local store each September, which was a lot considering you could buy a nice sweater for $10 back then), and a brand new, beautiful leased car (a yellow and white Chevy Impala convertible with an all-white interior that is a collectors item today). I had three jobs – one of which I actually worked at and two where I mostly showed up and exchanged basketball tickets for a paycheck. Again, I never thought much about these things. This was the way of the world, nothing exceptional.

I know there has been a lot of controversy lately about what the colleges do and don't do for their athletes. For the record, I think you could solve a lot of issues if student athletes were financially compensated fairly and above board. With all the computer technology and all the bright accountants we have, there's no reason we can't come up with a system for remunerating these talented and dedicated young men and women. Look at the simple economics. Room, board and tuition – especially for those playing on first-tier and championship teams – does not cover the opportunity cost that players take on by going to play at a university. I'm not at all under valuing the opportunity of a free ride student-athletes receive. But for the price athletes pay in fatigue, risk of injury, lack of focus on school and grades and, in many cases, missed opportunities to play money ball in Europe, South America, Canada or even China, there should be some form of gain sharing with the individuals who make it happen. My position on all this began to change when I saw the NCAA coaches salaries explode. Suddenly there were scores of multi-million dollar salaries and long-term contracts. Even the schools top administrators were blushing and questioning the decisions. It was then I realized college sports truly is a very big cash driven supply and demand business; based on cash in and cash out and the all important reality " you tend to get what you negotiate and not always what you deserve."

Ninety-nine percent of student athletes do not go any further in their sports playing careers after college. Yet they spend four years bringing in money to their schools in the form of ticket sales, alumni donations and media coverage that raises the schools admissions appeal. Do some players bring in more money than others? Sure, but there is certainly a formula we can devise that will give everyone a fair share. You can pool and apportion money to the workers that brought that money in. The NCAA is like any cartel that sets the rules; it won't change until pressure is brought to bear; like players not showing up for the final four. But I believe someone has to realize its about power and money – especially because the players who are hurt the worst by current policies are often minorities and those from the lower economic classes who may have few personal resources to draw upon once their college years are behind them.

If anybody has the ability to say "the system worked," it should be me. I came out a winner. But many come out losers. Typically, losers have no voice. That's why I believe it should be up to me and to those like me to give them one.

* * *

Of course, over 50 years ago, my 17-year-old self gave not a thought to the moral, ethical and economic dilemmas posed by being a student athletics. Why would I? I only thought about playing and winning. After all, winning was pretty much all Gov and I had known in the 15 years we had been together, perfecting our on-court dialogue like twins with a secret language all our own.

In truth, I was probably expecting nothing but accolades for winning once I got to the Big Ten. But things would not turn out exactly as I had anticipated.

In my first game against Butler University, I scored 26 points in front of a sold-out crowd, and I was thrilled. But, to my astonishment, Howie Braun, an assistant coach, called me over and said, "That was horrible. All you colored guys know is jumping and shooting. You won't play here doing that." He said that, in order for me to hold on to a starting role, he wanted me to get 10-plus assists and 10-plus rebounds. He shut me off when I said I'd been a shooter and scorer and a winner all my life. On one hand, Braun had a case: He would have preferred the starters scoring 80 to 85 points overall and paying more attention to building a team rather than scoring 100 points in a whirlwind. I did not realize at the time – but would later – that I should have spent less time dunking and shooting the ball and more time making others better players. With Gov, I had never had to worry about this; we just got the job done.

Braun may have had the right message, but the way he communicated it felt all wrong. The vehemence with which he took his frustration out on me that night made me wonder if there was more to it. Govoner and I were the first two Blacks to play basketball for Illinois and there probably weren't more than a dozen of us in the entire Big Ten Conference. Was some of Braun's irate delivery due to the fact that a number of white all-state players and "Mr. Basketballs" from Illinois, Indiana and Iowa were taking a back seat to Gov and me? I didn't know, but it crossed my mind.

In the end, we would have many triumphs, yet we never did develop into the team we should have been. Our head coach was, at this point in his career, past his peak and had quit working as hard as he had before. There were so many gifted players on our team, but also independent-minded ones. It would have taken a 24/7 effort and a leader of Herculean strength to handle the reins.

* * *

It didn't take long after my arrival on campus to understand the system. We were the first Blacks to make the team and play varsity ball; it became clearer each day that Illinois wanted me for basketball and little else. Over my years in school, I came to realize that too many athletes want to be placed in classes that are often less than challenging. I would walk into the Sports Office, and they would hand me a curriculum for the semester. I knew their plan was to keep things simple and keep us getting grade point averages that would enable us to keep playing basketball. My head was swirling most of the time and I'd push back too seldom, though when I did things would be fixed. I mistakenly thought the academics could always come later. The one thing about Illinois was that the schoolwork was no joke. You either studied and made the grades or you went home. The GPA standards were high and never did I ask for or receive any latitude with grades. Both Gov and I have always been extremely proud to have graduated on time with good grades. When young athletes ask me today about attending, I tell them be prepared to work – not just get by.

It was assumed, however – not by me, but by everyone around me – that all athletes would end up in education as coaches. The degree I left the U of I with was in education with a minor in science and coaching. But along the way, after undergrad I took many courses in economics and pre-law at schools like Bradley and Roosevelt University of Chicago, and later University of Detroit and Wharton. I remember Gov also had this yen for a more well-rounded education. He once signed up for an advanced world history course known around campus to be especially difficult. I watched him study like he never studied before, and I saw him pull it off with honors. In those days every adult was saying over and over to us that education would be the key. I was fully aware from watching my parents that reading was empowerment and that people had put their lives on the line to make certain their children had access to quality education. Spike Lee said recently, "Today's generation equates education with acting white, and acting and talking ignorant with acting Black, and they wear this act like a badge of honor. They say things like, 'I'm ghetto, I live for rap, I'm ghetto.' What they are, he said, is just ignorant." I couldn't agree more with Spike; college students earn millions of dollars more in a lifetime and the economic and social power to help others in need. The educated live and operate on the top of life's pyramid with few exceptions. I'll confess to idolizing sports stars as a child; my closest friends and family were intolerant of the drug scene and the so-called gangster culture. I was always being reminded that slavery was in our past as were the unlawful acts of reading and writing.

I knew we were smart, and I wasn't worried at all about our futures. But looking back I realize that we were the lucky ones. Dozens of Black student-athletes just dropped out along the way. The pressures of integration can be overwhelming, especially when so many of us spent our most critical developmental years in really bad segregated schools. My Uncle Bob was very smart, with superior basketball talents; he and Bill Penelton, also very smart, were potentially all-star division I players, but to this day, I blame educational apartheid for damaging their development and wasting their talents. Aside from being solid people and superior athletes, both could well have become top lawyers, physicians, or educators if it were not for quota systems and our countries "separate and (so called) equal" school situation. My friend Sam Johnson, who attended Lincoln School with me, was another casualty. A wonderful athlete, Sam never felt legitimate or confident anywhere but on the playing field. He stumbled through high school and immediately began a steep descent, spending several years in mental institutions and becoming just one of many tragic stories of those times. I blame educational apartheid for damaging the development and wasting the talents of many very smart young men and countless others like them.

Socially, Black athletes were seldom invited into the University of Illinois campus culture. There were only a few dorms in which we could live. The first few years, Gov and I had to live in an Army barracks on the parade ground. We would often have to go across the tracks into the Black community to get meals and haircuts.

This was the way things were and I accepted it. I learned, literally, to keep my head down and keep moving forward while avoiding traveling alone. When I go back to the University of Illinois as a proud alumni, I walk around the beautiful campus and in a very real sense it is like I am seeing it for the first time. To this day, I wonder what it would have been like to have a "real" undergraduate lifestyle. I wish I had gone to fancy events at the stately Student Union, or been invited into a dormitory or a major fraternity where the different parties were going on. But except for the small, segregated, under-capitalized Greek organizations, we could only dream because it was never to be.

Like water running downhill, however, Gov and I were the quiet commandos; we always found a path. We found people who liked and accepted us as people first with no labels. In our quest for friendships and recreation, we even discovered a local brothel, run by a madam my uncle knew from the South Side of Chicago, and made friends with the beautiful young ladies who worked there. The young ladies enjoyed hanging out with us between interludes with their usual, much older white clientele. We enjoyed the friendships, the food and the music. You can imagine the kind of scandal that might ensue today if star college athletes were found regularly frequenting a "house of ill repute." But there was little danger, back then, that anyone was going to know what Gov and I did in our off hours. Because the simple fact was that no one cared or bothered to inquire. No one ever said, "Hey guys, how was your weekend?" They didn't ask, and of course we didn't tell.

At the U of I, I didn't find the time to socialize much with co-eds and seldom dated. But ultimately I did meet and spend time with a young Black lady who was a very positive influence in my college life. She came from a very solid middle-class background – her father was a teacher in East St. Louis – and we became close friends. I learned a lot from her and enjoyed her refreshing candor. Even though her father was wary of the fact that I was an athlete, we remained friends. Later in life, she became an assistant dean, and the lessons I learned from this beautiful 18-year-old and her family were ones I have never forgotten.

One of my happiest moments in college was being elected captain of the university's varsity basketball team at the age of 19. The athletic director told the media: "This election was an acknowledgement of trust and leadership from every person associated with the Illinois basketball program." I must admit, I was nervous because of the excitement surrounding the honor and all the attention I was receiving. The first person I called was my dad. He understood more than I did at the time how significant this would be later in life. He told me he was proud and closed by saying, "Now go out and earn it. Prove them right."

I can't explain the rush I felt. But even this simple achievement was dashed by racial insensitivity. Right off, two of the assistant coaches looked at each other in my presence and asked, "How are we going to explain this vote?" They seriously asked me, "How would you feel about stepping aside?" This was followed by a private meeting in which the top assistant coach explained the pressures of the job to me and offered to extend the offer to one of my white teammates, under the premise that the state of Illinois and "my people" would applaud my good judgment. To this I quickly said, "No, thanks!"

Within 24 hours, this same coach realized that one of the honors bestowed upon the newly elected Illinois varsity basketball captain was to escort the Illinois High School State Tournament Queen to the annual state championship tournament. He said, "Imagine a 17-year-old, white beauty queen holding hands, smiling and being photographed for the next day's newspaper with a 'colored.' It just wouldn't be right." For good measure, he added, "For years to come, this young woman will be embarrassed and maybe permanently scarred."

I didn't budge. I escorted the young lady and no one said boo. Many years later, she showed up at the invitation of the owner (me) to a Harlem Globetrotters game at Madison Square Garden. I was in the second year of my ownership and very honored. After all the years, I wanted to asked this former Illinois beauty queen, Jeanie Evens, from Aurora, Illinois, two questions: Did she even remember that infamous night? And, if so, how she felt? Looking as beautiful as she had years earlier, she said she was thrilled and had the time of her life. In the photographs taken of her as the teenage queen-elect that night, she looked radiant and beautiful. For all these years I have never forgotten her poise and never regretted the experience, which was to become a defining moment in my life. She and her attorney mother were both righteous people of great character. Needless to say, even though this whole episode had upset me deeply on a personal level, it made me more aware of the potential for good and bad in people and of how the ill-conceived judgments of some leaders are windows into their own ignorance, self-interests and personal issues. As I look back on those days and all the shit we put up with, I'll never understand why two players of our status and statistical records aren't unanimously inducted into the school's list of greatest athletic pioneers and achievers. Imagine the difficulty and price paid to play at all-star levels while working to exceed all social and academic standards with one arm tied behind our backs and facing the obstacles thrown at you every doggone day.

To this day, I struggle with my emotions about the racial incidents that occurred and attitudes that prevailed during my high school and college years. Yes, there was a boatload of genuine prejudice and willful ignorance. Yet I believe there were many basically good and innocent people who were conditioned by the bad behavior that was widely practiced and rarely questioned. I didn't understand or appreciate the times my teammates sat in the front of a restaurant with their parents and girlfriends while I watched from the kitchen. But worse than that was the fact that no one came to me and said, "Hey, this is a bad situation. Maybe we shouldn't come back to this restaurant anymore." I don't understand why these guys I loved so much didn't think, "Wait, this is happening to a great ballplayer – to our friend." Did they think, "That's the way it is and we can't help it," or "This is the way it's supposed to be?" This has haunted me for such a long time, and finally, not long ago, I brought it up to one of those guys and he apologized. He said he just didn't realize, didn't understand the depths of it, the impact it had.

I do recall with great fondness some exceptions to the "code" of segregationist behavior. Jerry Colangelo, a teammate who transferred from Kansas and later in life became owner of the Phoenix Suns and Arizona Diamondbacks, was probably the first white teammate who seriously discussed the flaws in the social system with Gov and I from his perspective. Jerry was a unique person and a breath of fresh air.

He never seemed to want to distance himself from us after basketball. We were always welcome to come to his frat house to meet, study and listen to music. He had this obsession at the time for Frank Sinatra and Dean Martin tunes, which Gov and I never quite appreciated. But we loved the guy anyway. Colangelo was and remains truly authentic – a life-long friend who has never forgotten where we all came from or what the phrase "team" means. I've yet to meet a professional basketball or baseball player, especially Black stars, who didn't cite Jerry as their all-time favorite owner.

I also remember traveling to a game against the University of Kentucky during a year in which they held the nation's No. 1 ranking. Because Illinois had Black players, we couldn't play Kentucky in Lexington, so they scheduled us at the Fairgrounds in Louisville. While we were there, the entire team decided to go to a movie. Gov and I were turned away at the door because of the no-Blacks policy. Immediately several teammates offered to leave with us – including our team student manager, Dennis Swanson, who raised holy hell with the theater manager and staff and threatened to shut the place down. Most of our teammates looked on and were in total shock. But since Gov and I had had these experiences several years earlier, we knew our time would come on the basketball court.

By halftime in the game we were doing great, and I had already scored 19 points. Kentucky's Hall of Fame coach was furious. He was all over the officials, trying to intimidate them. Five minutes into the second half, I was out of the game after picking up a fifth foul. For the rest of the game, police were stationed behind our bench. Gov was given the perfect 18-foot final shot with just seconds remaining. No one in the history of college basketball was more prepared to take what was, for him, a routine shot. If he had made it, it would have been the biggest upset of the year and our careers. He missed though, and as we left the floor, the Kentucky band played a chorus of "Bye Bye Blackbird." Still, we had done our job and helped awaken the South to a new day in college sports. Plus, I won't ever forget my hero, Dennis Swanson, and that moment of racial solidarity at that movie theatre. (By the way, Mr. Swanson today is a close friend with Oprah Winfrey and is frequently cited by her as giving Oprah her first big television break that opened the doors to her fame and history-making career). To this I'm not the least bit surprised.

It was during these college years that I also met the Reverend Jesse Jackson, a quarterback out of North Carolina who had been recruited by the University of Illinois football team. While it was the beginning of a lifelong friendship, Jesse was already light years ahead of us. He was different and special. He was extremely articulate, even then. He could quote the Bible with ease; and the Constitution as well as he could quote yesterday's newspaper. He knew there were harsh realities ahead for us to deal with during and after college. He was smarter than most of the coaches and wouldn't allow them to threaten him, pep talk him or con him. Jesse was always measured and calm, but he could not accept the system at Illinois. He left the school and became a standout student-athlete and all-star quarterback at North Carolina A & T. His actions and astute assessments of social situations at an early age still amaze me. This is a man who has never gotten the credit he deserves. He and I are still close, and he spoke with passion, wisdom and authority at my dad's funeral recently.

* * *

By the time I was a senior, I was struggling to figure out what my next basketball role would be – or if there was going to be one. I was first-team All-Big Ten, and third- and fourth-team All-American. My game averages, I'm told, were: 16 points, nine assists and eight rebounds. While I had a very good college record, I did not attract big professional offers. My biggest compliment came at the annual holiday tournament in Los Angeles competing against California, West Virginia (which featured Jerry West), Michigan and several other ranked teams. Illinois finished third, losing to tourney and NCAA champion California. The all-tournament first team had four future NBA all-stars and myself- I'd averaged 26 point and ran like a beachboy in that fresh California air – one writer picked me as most likely to achieve professional stardom.

I remember telling reporters then that I wasn't sure it mattered. I was already eyeing another kind of goal. I was just 20 years of age, and I wanted to be the leading scorer and point guard for a Fortune 500 company. I had began exploring possibilities two years earlier, as a result of meeting more and more alumni and finding out what they were doing in their careers. I saw students beginning to go out on internships for a semester. I wondered what that was like and wished I could do the same. I knew I had a lot to offer an employer. I was intelligent, accomplished and goal driven. But when I applied for a position at Ralston-Purina, the personnel department said they "knew a guy at the YMCA" that could use me. I hadn't gone to school for that.

During my junior year, Kroger, the supermarket chain, had come onto campus promoting their intern management-training program. They were going to be testing applicants. The night before I was to take their test, I asked a young lady administering the exam to have dinner with me. She had anticipated that I might ask for a copy of the test and when I didn't, she still handed me one.

The next day, I felt guilty and purposely missed a single question – I didn't want a perfect score to arouse suspicion. But I missed *only* one.

Several times I phoned Kroger's headquarters to see how I had done, but I could not get an answer other than, "We're still processing the exams." Finally, a reply came via mail. They had room for only a few well-qualified students – translation in those days meaning white, male students – with the best test scores. My test score fell below their standards. "Please apply again." If I'd had a crystal ball and known how successful I would be in the business world, all of this would have been beyond ironic. But at the time it was just hurtful.

As graduation approached, it became more and more clear to me that none of the Fortune 500 were about to throw their doors open wide. My future was uncertain. College was behind me, though, and if I didn't take an over-abundance of fond memories with me, I was clear that it had been a period of important development in my life. I had the sense, even then, that the stage was set for my life's dreams to be realized. I was ready... for something, though I still wasn't quite sure what.

Harlem Globetrotters owner Abe Saperstein had stayed in touch while I played at Illinois, and I was aware that a stint with the Globetrotters could lead to a pro career. By the time I graduated, though, the Harlem Globetrotters were so popular and so good, joining them seemed an impossibility. Abe did invite me to play in the Harlem Globetrotter-College All-Star 26-game series, the Chicago game was billed as Abe's test for an all new format, but I balked at losing my amateur status for a $50 per game payment that was being offered.

I knew I was turning my back on the prospect of playing for sellout crowds, not to mention risking the loss of Abe's favor. But I thought there were other ways into the pros. I decided to set my sights on the Olympics.

4 GLOBE TROTTING

The 1960 United States Men's Olympic Basketball Team competed in the Games of the XVII Olympiad. The team, coached by California Golden Bears coach Pete Newell, won its games by an astonishing average of over 42 points. The team, elected to the Naismith Memorial Basketball Hall of Fame as a unit in 2010, is considered by many to be America's best amateur basketball team ever. Its members included Cincinnati's Oscar Robertson, West Virginia's Jerry West, Ohio State's Jerry Lucas, Purdue's Terry Dischinger and Indiana's Walt Bellamy.

You will notice the name Mannie Jackson is nowhere on the roster.

Since I was named All-Big Ten, and mentioned on all the All-American teams, I was optimistic about my chances. I had played against and had made first-team all-star and all-conference teams with every player on the 1960 team, except Oscar. I had played well in an unofficial regional workout, and expected an invitation to the final trials. However, while waiting for a plane ticket to arrive, I learned I had not been selected. It seemed to me I was suddenly eliminated without an opportunity to actively compete. This shocked me to the point where I temporarily lost complete respect and focus on sports.

Part of me feared that maybe basketball wasn't at all fair, and even the best situation wasn't going to furnish me with any fascinating opportunities in the immediate future. But part of me was still hoping the Globetrotters or maybe the NBA would do what the Olympic Committee hadn't – just give me a chance.

After a long wait, the mail brought something after all. I felt extremely honored to receive an invitation to join the New York Tuck Tapers, a National Industrial League team.

The National Industrial Basketball League was originally founded in 1947 to enable mill workers a chance to compete in basketball. By this point, it had major teams from coast to coast. Its games were played at a high level by elite former All-Americans and standout student-athletes from major universities all over the country.

The Industrial League had an inordinate number of outstanding Black players, because the NBA was still largely segregated. Although it wasn't a publicly acknowledged policy, and some may choose to deny it today, everyone close to the NBA at the time knew that the recently "integrated" eight-team league operated under a quota system, with two or three Blacks per team. (The exception was Hall of Fame coach Red Auerbach and his World Champion Boston Celtics, who were clearly more interested in winning than in color schemes.)

The Tuck Tapers were owned by the Technical Tape Corporation of New Rochelle, New York, a company that dealt in bulk sales of pressure-sensitive tapes – masking, cellophane and the stronger stuff. As a National Industrial League team, the New York Tapers offered an advantage that most sports organizations did not. Many of the athletes were there exclusively for basketball, but Technical Tape owner Paul Cohen identified certain players he felt had the aptitude and personality to be of value in a business sense and offered them jobs outside the game. (I discovered recently that several former All-Americans who joined the league in those days are still active executives with their companies.) I was fortunate to be one of those players selected.

While playing for the team, I would work on the national customer service desk, handling marketplace product problems from all over the country. Later, I'd be assigned to work in sales support in Manhattan as a training "shadow" to Gus Platto, the company's oldest and top producer. I liked the notion of beginning a career that combined high-level business exposure with the opportunity to play some great domestic and international basketball. I was happy that I would finally get the business training I hadn't received at Illinois.

I was also eager to head to New York, to make my mark, and to thumb my nose at the prejudiced NBA. I couldn't wait to play against all the former Big Ten players with the Celtics, Knicks and the 76ers. But what I discovered in the streets of New York was shocking: There were scores of Black athletes, and most of these guys had nowhere to go. After a week in the big city, I quickly realized how really good Gov and I were competing against the country's best players and how fortunate I was to have been raised in a small southern Illinois town and not in this congested metropolis. This was to be a true love-hate adjustment. New York was going to take some getting used to.

I almost didn't stay a Taper for long. Just before formal Globetrotter tryout camp, my old friend Abe Saperstein called me and insisted that I should at least come back and give the Trotters a hard look. I had a great job and a super boss, but since Gov had been released by the Tapers and was going in for a tryout, I took the ride. As good as Gov had played, I felt it wouldn't be long before I to would be released. Playing on these teams was like playing in today's NBA. The competition in the Industrial League was brutal. Everyone was pedigreed and very accomplished. The players in that league would easily have filled several 10-12 team rosters in today's NBA.

I could write an entire book on that process and all the talent that showed up at the South Side St. Anselm gym for the Globetrotter tryout. It was a musty old place with bleacher seating. Just about every legend from Trotter history, the media, current team members, many household names, and players from every part of the world were there. I think there were nearly 200 people there when Abe finally ordered the doors locked and rolled the balls out with absolutely no preamble. As it turned out, both Gov and I played great, and it was quickly noted we could be the main rookie attractions. After four hours of really hard work, we were given contracts on the spot. But when I called Paul Cohen to tell him where I was, he said, "Congratulations, but there's too much here in New York for you to turn your back on." Then he added, "With your skills you can always just play basketball."

I was undecided, so he said to come in Monday morning and we'd finish our conversation in his office. He was a great salesman. We talked on Monday, and I committed. He'd already had my business cards printed up. From that moment, with two brand new suits and four shirts and ties from Mr. Cohen's tailor on North Avenue in New Rochelle, and $3,000 cash in my pocket, I was very happy and ready to give my job my best effort. At 21 years old, this turned out to be one of my best career decisions ever.

Suddenly, New York showed me her other face. The city seemed very glamorous and loaded with many big opportunities. To be competitive and respected in that environment was ultimately to become my biggest sports achievement. There is nothing in the world – absolutely nothing – like being a recognized sports personality in that town. Even if it's just for a moment.

My other good fortune was that the Technical Tape Corporation had purchased a two-hour television time block to play all their Friday night home games from the old 27th Street Regiment Armory on local area TV. I was promised that if I stayed with the team I would be featured in advertisements as the future of the league with the Big Ten pedigree, and that my customer service department would receive special mention. Back in those days it was a major event to see a Black person on television, even in New York City. To me this was all so cool – a dream situation.

Fortunately, all these great recruiting promises were made to me before the coaches saw me struggle to keep up with the likes of Jim Daniels, Frank Keith – both five or six years older than I and amazing stars – as well as Ed Willis and Carolina's Lee Schaefer.

I was playing point guard, a position also known as the playmaker or "the ball-handler." Basically, a point guard is expected to run the team's offense by controlling and distributing the ball – that is, making sure that it gets to the right players at the necessary moment. But the fact was that I had no preparation for the half-court game the Tapers wanted, and I really struggled for meaningful playing time even in games in which I'd start.

My best friend, LeRoy Wright, our 6-foot-11 defensive stopper from the College of the Pacific, told me my problem was an East Coast versus West Coast style thing. Others would say a Black point guard wasn't ever going to be a point guard scorer unless he was an Oscar Robertson. They said only a white guy could keep that job on a losing team and here I was a Black guy trying to quarterback a losing team with great talent.

One week, another guard from the San Francisco Investors showed up in our locker room. I knew the truth: He was there because I wasn't doing as well as expected. It was confusing in many ways, but essentially I was okay with it. I was young, and just needed experience and time.

Coach Hank Rosenstein summed it up. "Mannie," he said, "you are 21 and no one has ever taught you right from wrong, or how to really play this game. You jump higher than anyone on the team and run faster. If we turned you loose you'd be the league's top scorer, but we'd lose most of our games. You are a big-time scorer that has to have the ball all the time. You have a great unstoppable shot but you have shamefully weak ball-handling and passing skills. Your athleticism puts you in the top 10 percent of professional players, but your overall game is in the bottom 10 percent. That makes you a nice guy with good size and skills, but a liability." The point guard is the toughest position played at the professional level; there's this constant pressure of speed and decision making and an absolute requirement to think "set the team up and pass first." All this takes place while you are guarding the best athlete on the floor- most often the opposing point guard.

This was the essence of a conversation at St. Peter's College following a loss against an NBA team. I had scored 15-second half points and our Tuck Taper team had lost by over 20 points. I really couldn't see his argument at first, because from my standpoint I did what I had always been hired to do, move the team fast, stretch the floor, and score points.

Rosenstein advised me to take a week away from the team, and ask Mr. Cohen for a pay raise and a bigger job in the office. "Mr. Cohen likes you," he explained. "If he says okay, come back to me and I believe I can teach you how to play.

"When I watch your game," he added, "you have nothing to distinguish you but the scoring and the fact that you are fun to watch. I can teach you the game and I believe you can, at some point, make better passing decisions and eventually play defense. I know I can get you ready for next year, but first I have to convince you to forget about scoring, and then maybe we'll have something to build on."

Forget about scoring? My head was swimming. I remembered Howie Braun chewing me out at the University of Illinois, but this was different. For the first time that I could remember, I had gotten a negative performance appraisal and actually felt energized. I knew Rosenstein was right. I knew something was wrong with the way I played the game, but I couldn't cover up my flaws (which every player has at every level) to save my game. I had been faking success, even when the team was losing, with my hustle and scoring. I reminded myself about that "bigger job" in the offing. Two things were certain: This wasn't about race, and no one was out to get me or see me fail. Thank you, Mr. Rosenstein. (He later played me a lot and I had a great experience.) I made the transformation and I was no doubt a much better team mate; had I played close to this new way in college Illinois would have competed strongly for a national title and who knows what else or great I could have helped others on the team become.

Still, on some level, the truth about my basketball game was hard to hear. I remember walking into my favorite nightspot, Small's Paradise in Harlem, that night, after leaving my car double-parked on 125th Street. I sat eating alone and feeling like everyone I met or looked at had been in the locker room listening to Hank call me out. I left the club at about 2:00 a.m., standing alone in the greatest city in the world wondering what's next. For a moment in time I was lost. My beautiful new car, my custom-made three-piece suit, my freshly minted wavy slick Harlem haircut, and my "Boston roll" of cash ($100 in singles and twenties covered with two brand new crisp hundred-dollar bills) couldn't hide the damage to my ego and pride. This was a new experience, and for a moment in my dream life I found myself contemplating a face-saving honorable detour. To top it off, I'd watched Gov play with the Trotters a week earlier in Teterboro, New Jersey. I was missing Edwardsville and realizing how important that little town was to my life. I missed my mom, my dad, my sister and everything else. I realized the balance of life: Good fortunes in New York can take you to the moon; conversely, the downs are staggering. Everything in this town seemed exaggerated.

Oh well, I thought, it's a beautiful night in the city, and things are just starting to happen. I could drive to Brooklyn's Red Hook District housing projects, where I'll surely see a couple of my teammates hanging out, as well as an ex-girlfriend. The music will be cool and there will be plenty to eat: barbecue, some greens, cornbread, fried chicken, fried chitlins, sweet potato pies and whatever else I decided to pick up along the way. This was the scene at the usual celebrity gathering and $5 rent party. There was nothing like it. I loved the people I'd meet there, from Broadway and Apollo theater folks to the sports crowd from Madison Square Garden. The drive would take 35 to 40 minutes if I didn't get lost, and I would probably spend the night. It occurred to me that if I were in Edwardsville, I would be 15 minutes from the K-bar in Newport-Madison, Illinois and I could catch Ike and

Tina Turner's first show. (I once went on stage after being introduced and played the alto saxophone, which was a horrible mistake. I'm sure I looked as foolish as I felt, but it made for many good laughs.)

At home, my mom, my sister and Aunt Dee were my favorite dance partners and we could go until daybreak without stopping. Now, tonight, there seemed to be so many different choices. There was a party in Spanish Harlem, I realized, just 10 minutes away. The smart and beautiful Rosario Cruz, a dispatcher from our Bronx factory, would be there with her family. Ever since I gave them front-row tickets to a Tapers game, I was treated like kin and I appreciated it because that meant I'd be safe and looked out for. The food at this party would be sparse, but the dancing and music would be over the top. At this party, I could dance and flirt with Rosario without anyone caring or trying to talk basketball. The language barrier would be an asset in this case. As I pulled away in my car, I searched for WABC on the radio to cruise to the sounds of the Dells, the Teenagers, Heartbeats, Five Satins, Sam Cooke, the Drifters, the Temptations and my favorite then, the Chantels.

* * *

At the time I did not fully appreciate that I was receiving a wake-up call preparing me to enter a new phase of my young life. I stayed with the Tuck Tapers that season, and for the first time I was actually beginning to learn the game at which I'd always been told I'd excelled. By season's end, I was a pretty confident businessperson and playing the best basketball of my life.

Now what? The NBA, as I said, was still largely segregated. The word was that even the great Bill Russell had to be traded after the draft –

because of his race – by the St. Louis Hawks to Boston for Ed McCauley and Kansas All-American Clyde Lovellette. In those days, in virtually every major city across the country, just as in New York, there were hundreds of really great Black players unemployed. People ask me all the time how I felt about this, and I always have said I realized from the get-go just how laughable, stupid and damaging prejudice can be – all because of fear, greed and ignorance. No matter how you rationalize it, prejudice always falls into one of those categories – and we are all victimized by it. But I refuse to worry about it affecting my love for a good game of basketball. I reached this conclusion because the people who mattered to me always understood this laughable but sad situation.

The most ridiculous rationale for limiting Black players was that somehow Blacks weren't smart enough to play the cerebral white style of basketball. As Earl Lloyd, the first African-American basketball player in the NBA and a longtime friend, recounted in his book, *Moonfixer*: Harold Hunter, a strong and talented point guard from North Carolina College, believed he was passed over because the power brokers didn't want to believe a person of color could think or lead or handle pressure on the basketball court (any more than they could envision a Black football player as a quarterback.) I could never understand how segregationists rationalized the championship play of the all-Black New York Rens, arguably the greatest basketball team of their time, or how they explained the Harlem Globetrotters' repeated victories over the all-white league champion Lakers.

Just as ludicrous was the notion that white parents would never want their kids to admire and emulate Black sports heroes. Kids, Black and white alike, should never be deprived of heroes. I find it a sad and telling that Earl Lloyd also wrote in his book that people often asked him if he had planned a professional basketball career. His answer was, "Are you kidding me? How can you plan to pursue a career in an arena where you see no one before you who looked like you or thought like you?"

I could go on and on listing outrageously stupid premises for prejudice in pro sports. But eventually things evolved – in part because of money. The quota system in the NBA changed when a handful of enlightened capitalists realized it was no longer in their economic self-interest to turn their backs on the moral and constitutional arguments put forth by civil rights activists and by the game's courageous pioneers, both Black and White.

But for me, at this juncture in my life, the NBA was neither a realistic nor an appealing option. With the Tuck Tapers' season successfully behind me, I contacted Abe Saperstein. Although the Globetrotters were beginning to clown around a little bit more for the crowds they drew, Abe continued to assemble a breathtakingly serious stable of world-class basketball talent. All you have to do is look at the rosters. By the late '60s and early '70s, over half a dozen Trotters from the same era and team had become NBA All-Stars (including Wilt Chamberlain, Walters Dukes, Woody Saulsberry, Andy Johnson, Joe Buckhalter, Connie Hawkins and Willie Gardner). I'm guessing that at one point Abe had on his payroll 90 percent of the best players in the world. By 1959, he had already done two full-length feature films, and had built the industry's strongest brand. He had all the markets in every city covered, and was taking the Globetrotters international in a big way.

I apologized to Abe for standing him up in pre-season, and told him Hank Rosenstein had turned me into the strongest player I had ever been. The only thing was... I now wanted more than anything else to be a businessman.

Abe very slowly talked about our connection of many years and then told me, "I want to help you achieve your dream." Then he asked me, "Where else but with the Globetrotters will you see the world *and* the future of business?" I listened for several minutes, and he made sense.

At the time, some people questioned Abe's motives. Some said he was stockpiling more and more talent for the future American Basketball League. Some also claimed he was not paying his players fairly. But I tell you, Abe Saperstein was not a super rich man because the economics were simply not in the game at that time, neither for the Trotters nor the NBA. One can't honestly make a case that Saperstein held on to cash rather than pay the players because he was prejudiced and white. After all, how many multi-millionaire Harlem Rens were walking the streets? I always tell the cynics: Take your hats off and give the man his due. (That said, in my opinion, the Globetrotter asset owned by the Sapersteins just didn't translate into the big financial values it should have. For sure, Wilt Chamberlain, Marques Haynes, Meadowlark Lemon and certainly Goose Tatum made big incomes – but not today's staggering generational wealth.)

To me, Abe's caring and pride were obvious and, whatever his motives, I was in a win-win position. He said he had an important call to take, but he wanted me to obtain a passport and report to the team's Chicago headquarters. I hung up the phone and went to see Paul Cohen. All he would say as he barely looked over the reading classes on top of his nose was good luck, enjoy your vacation and he'd hold my job until I returned. I left the country soon thereafter for Europe, feeling strangely like he and Abe had struck some kind of deal.

* * *

As a proud new member of the Harlem Globetrotters, I was on Cloud Nine – or, more precisely, on an Alitalia jet to London and bound for 30-plus countries after that. In what seemed like a flick of a switch, I was sitting with some of the best players in the world: Goose Tatum, the template and the master from whom everything to do with entertainment in Globetrotter history was created; the team's newest star and showman, Meadowlark Lemon, who was proving to be legit and had already stolen the hearts of millions worldwide; and J.C. Gipson, who towered at 6-foot-9. Also there were 6-foot-5, 230-pound "weeping" Willie Thomas from Tennessee State, the team's power point guard; Hallie Bryant, the 6-foot-5 All-American guard from Indiana University; Murphy Summons, the 6-foot-6 Detroit street legend; and team leader, 6-foot-4 Tex Harrison.

As a group, my companions were wise, smart, cocky, sophisticated and, for the first time in my career, all Black. This particular team of Trotters was a proud bunch, with good reason. They were gifted individually and as a unit. To me, this was a representative group of the hundreds of Black players segregation had left behind.

Discrimination caused the Trotters' talent pool to grow incredibly over the years. Our group would soon be joined (for some summer fun and butt kicking) by 7-foot-2 Wilt Chamberlain, Seton Hall's 7-foot Walter Dukes, 6-foot-9 Hall of Famer Connie Hawkins, and New York City leaping legend, "Jumpin" Jackie Jackson. I don't know firsthand how amazing Jackie Jackson was or could have been, because I only saw him a couple times in his prime. In my entire time being involved with the team, a span of over 40 years, Jackie is the most fabled athlete in Globetrotter history. (Although, when I owned the Trotters, I had Mike Wilson, an absolute freak – and the current world's slam-dunk record holder – on one of my teams for seven years. His photograph and the hoop on which he set the world record are displayed on the second floor of the Naismith Memorial Basketball Hall of Fame in a place of honor near Hall of Famer Michael Jordan. I saw Mike Wilson slam-dunk with ease in Los Angeles, at the Forum, on a basketball hoop set at 12 1/2 feet. Our manager, Jimmy Poulus, measured incorrectly in a rush, thinking it was set at 12 feet.)

Abe and his scouts exploited fully the supply side of the free market. They knew "best in class" talent and knew the Trotters were a Black player's most viable option. Having said that, all the players who joined us only served to make our legacy more interesting. This group, post-integration alone, featured four Hall of Famers enshrined with the fabulous 2002 Hall of Fame team.

As a point guard on these early '60s teams I cannot remember – nor could Tex Harrison when I asked him – ever rehearsing a skit or routine. We scored points off fast breaks and in transition. In half court stacks we took cues from centers like J.C and Meadowlark and executed the fastest and the greatest motion offense I'd ever seen or been a part of. Watching Wilt or J.C. play the point was also an incredible show, particularly with the matchups and options they created. Even today, as a fan of the NBA and a Phoenix Suns season ticket holder, I watch NBA teams and I think, "This player would have been a fit for our team," or I see someone else and say to myself, "He couldn't have made it."

* * *

The first touring experience for me was enriched immeasurably because Abe decided to join the team. He made me one of the team's featured players and, as promised, spent a great deal of personal time with me. Photos of the two of us were taken in Paris, in Brussels, at the Berlin Wall, and at a former Polish concentration camp where I learned from Abe, who was Jewish, about the suffering of another race of people. I saw labor and death camps and heard the horror stories from eye witnesses and to this day I have never forgot the experience.

Mindful of my interest in business, Abe would talk to me for hours about how he promoted and marketed the team, and how he had made it one of the most famous brands in the world. I look back on it today and I appreciate his commitment as well as his savvy about both product branding and message branding. Forty years later, when I owned the team myself, I would dig deep to add sophistication to what he did naturally. In my view, Abe remains the most significant creative genius behind an immensely interesting sports and social experiment. Somehow, he and New York Rens founder Bob Douglas made the "urban style" unbeatable. Abe pioneered the fusion of sports and entertainment, and it was Abe's success that showcased to white America and the world the wildly talented Black player, thus debunking the myths and lies that were used to justify segregation. He helped put segregation in the light it deserved, uncovering decades of deception, fear and ignorance.

Abe would say: Tell the market you are the best and then be excellent. Be consistent. At every turn, remind them of your past (what you stand for and what you accomplished). He'd say pick your market (where you perform) carefully. And never ever forget who pays the bills. He repeated over and over, "We must be special, we are the State Department's ambassadors to the world. No one beats us and no one entertains better – that's why we continue to draw people from all walks of life all over the world."

Granted, sometimes Abe was inscrutable, kind of like a business visionary rather than a sports guy. When the team visited places that had never seen the game before, he'd chide me and others with statements like, "They may not always know what we say, but must never forget how we say it." Now go figure that out. He wanted the game to belong to everyone, as fun to watch as to play.

Abe's style had a great influence on the way I saw the business side of sports. He also made it obvious that he thought I was something more than just a player, and that there was a future for me in the organization beyond on-the-court basketball. I got along great with him because all I wanted was the experience, the education and the credentials. He showed me the numbers: In 1958 the team drew 4 million people worldwide (many of the games we played – rain or shine – on our tour were in soccer stadiums before 20,000-40,000 people), and most of the games were sell-outs.

We prepared ourselves every day to be able to play anyone and still entertain. We certainly were not what you would call overpaid. Nevertheless, I had a college teammate who was making just $8,800 a year as a starter in the NBA, and I was making more. Plus, Abe would often slip me extra cash after a game and say, "thank you." But to me, the Globetrotters salary was not the most relevant matter. What I was experiencing justified my decision to be happy and productive as a Globetrotter. (Besides, as my business partner Dennis Mathisen once told me, never count another man's money because if you are truly creating value, money will always follow value.)

When the team landed in London, it was the first time I had touched foreign soil. That remains a thrill frozen in time. We would eventually appear in many beautiful countries, including Russia and several Middle Eastern countries, from Lebanon to Libya, Iraq, Iran and Bahrain. We played their pick-up teams, their Olympic squads and their proud national teams. At every stop, the games were extremely serious contests, yet our victories usually came with ease and the fans loved it, in part because Meadowlark and J.C. were indomitable comedy masters. We would win, yet we always left opponents smiling and inviting us back.

The Globetrotters found a refreshingly different attitude toward race throughout most of Europe. I soon realized that, whether we liked it or not, to non-Americans we weren't Negroes, colored, or Black; we were America's greatest exported asset – entertainers, yes, but also role models for freedom and democracy who were living their own dreams. Yet, it would occur to me that all the adoration we were receiving could likely stop if most of these people immigrated to the United States and became racially frightened citizens. Just thinking about this concept would often give me a headache. I'd look around at the other guys for confirmation of my feelings but, except for Hallie Bryant, this thought didn't seem to bother or even occur to my teammates. I mentioned this once to Abe and he just smiled, wrote it down, and laughed.

Sometimes we would encounter significant racial animosity in countries with large U.S. military bases. Traveling abroad, my teammates and I could eat where we wanted and see whatever women we wanted. That sort of freedom caused several minor altercations with military personnel. But we were a no-nonsense entourage that was disarmingly capable of handling every situation. (I recall one incident where two rowdy, burly, ex-football-playing G.I.s lost consciousness in what seemed like a 30-second contest in front of an indifferent French night club crowd.) I would sometimes roll with J.C Gipson or Murphy Summons and, truthfully, you'd be a fool to mess with either of those characters. Murphy was a street-smart ghetto cowboy who carried both a big knife and a custom crafted pearl-handled Smith and Wesson pistol. J.C., a 6-foot-9, 290-pound giant, was a fearless bulldog and enforcer. He'd laugh and play, but no one dared to push him too far.

It was in Russia and, later, behind the Iron Curtain (a popular real estate term for Communist occupied territory in the '60s and '70s) that I found myself answering questions I had never publicly addressed before. I listened to myself defending democracy and capitalism to students who wanted to know if racism was as extreme in the United States as they had been told – and, if so, why was it tolerated in a so-called free society. They would ask me: "Why can't you vote?" and "Why is there segregated education?" They were fully aware of the unrest and social and political developments caused by implementation of the Fifteenth Amendment and Brown vs. Board of Education. They even had news articles and photographs showing the racial brutality of Sheriff Bull Connors in Birmingham, clashes in Selma, and the actions of Alabama's governor, George Wallace.

I responded by saying that, first and foremost, my country and its government were too often and for too long horrible examples of imperfect works in progress. I noted that the extreme beliefs of some people were counterproductive, mean-spirited and downright cruel, but that even stupidity was often tolerated in an open and free environment like America, to a point. In the end, I explained, the rule of constitutional law prevailed.

I told them of the Emmett Till story. I told them of my own dreams of escaping poverty and my boxcar home in Illmo, Missouri, and of my hopes of being wealthy and philanthropic. I talked about what I knew of the American political system: how it's supposed to work equally and fairly for everyone, thus allowing an ordinary person like Harry S. Truman, and other good people with differing points of view, to be in governing and leadership positions. I explained that a person like me could actually dream of being president. I talked about advocates of equality, like Martin Luther King, the Kennedy brothers, Adam Clayton Powell, Jesse Jackson, Rap Brown and Malcolm X. I talked about our capitalistic free-market system, where a Black child and boxcar dreamer like myself could one day become a professional athlete or a business executive like the few I'd met at Pepsi, Ford Motors and at Paul Cohen's Technical Tape Corporation. I told them about Black team owners Goose Tatum and Marques Haynes, and New York Rens owner Bob Douglas. I said that one day I might own an *Ebony* or *Jet* magazine, or even the Harlem Globetrotters.

My listeners just smiled then, as would I, and lowered their heads. I must admit that my amateur sociology lesson left me a little embarrassed, so I would quickly ask those in my audience what their dreams and hopes were, and whether they should have to leave their homeland to achieve them. I must say I surprised myself, and for the first time appreciated the power of talking out loud about one's opinions, dreams and aspirations.

In Eastern Europe, I often mingled with college students to exchange views and experiences. For that liberty, I once found myself in Abe's "dog house" and also in a Polish retention center for several hours. I guess exercising my freedom of speech and First Amendment rights was not always appreciated in the old Soviet satellite countries. I might have been better off, or at least safer, listening to jazz and blues, smoking weed (which I never did), getting drunk, or flirting with their young women.

* * *

All of us loved to play our international games, but we also loved the always highly competitive United States College All-Star Series. My participation in this series marked the second time I played with Hall of Famer Connie Hawkins. The experience was magical, all of it: the crowds, Connie and the competition. I once watched Gov Vaughn knock down eight or nine straight shots from 20 to 25 feet in the closing minutes of a physically tough game before a sold-out Chicago stadium crowd against the nation's top college seniors. He was later named the tour's MVP. That was a very special night for my family and me. I'd never seen anything like it, before or since.

For all of this excitement, however, Globetrotter life could sometimes be boring and debilitating. In those days, a typical player played 250 games a year. Much of our travel was by bus, leaving from one arena late at night to be in another city for the next afternoon game or promotion. Sometimes it was so much fun you hardly noticed the time passing or the travel, but other times you did.

I'm often asked how those "Chuck" Converse All-Star shoes held up through several hundred games in some very odd playing conditions. Well, cardboard and thick socks, along with very strong, calloused feet, strong ankles and dependable knees were essential. I loved everything about those shoes, but getting used to playing almost barefoot in those thin soles was simply a right of Harlem Globetrotter passage. (My first pair of all-leather handmade dress shoes was crafted in Milan, Italy. They were a work of art: absolutely beautiful to look at and kid glove-like to wear. Being raised in the U.S. shoe capital near St Louis, I knew great shoes, since Grandfather Jackson maintained the largest and coolest selection of Stacy Adams in the area. I told Meadowlark after I saw the price tag, I couldn't afford the shoes, but he said, "Hey young squirrel, you can when you hang out with me." I wore those shoes with pride for nearly 20 years.)

My goal was to be featured as the team's star competitive player, a fancy dribbler and finisher – the latter meaning that I was expected to explode off the floor and complete plays with spectacular slam-dunks. I can tell you one thing for certain: being a Globetrotter athlete is one of most physically demanding jobs in all of sports. This is especially true when losing is not an option and every show or improvisation has to be perfectly executed. The Trotters put on a unique show; there has never been, nor will there ever be, anything like it. The show is a fast-paced situation comedy built around the game of basketball, the most difficult game on the planet. In all cases the reams or skits are built as parody of the very serious and sometimes methodical game of roundball. The hallmark of the team is skill, first and foremost, then comedy, and precision execution. Although it varies from year to year, there are always at least eight players on the roster with the pedigrees and skills needed to compete against the best in the world.

I soon found out what those very challenging roles will do to a person's legs and feet over time. The relentless wear and tear was like nothing I've ever known or seen. My body clock told me very early that mine would not be a long career. It might have been shorter than it was, because I wasn't internally driven or motivated to train that much. If it were not for Hallie Bryant, I might have been like the others and never worked as hard between games, preferring to shop, sleep or just relax. Fortunately, my friend Hallie – a big, strong, tough guard who, like me, lived for the big games and the big shots – got me to train and practice regularly. (He had been an army officer stationed in Asia and, to pass the time on outpost assignments, he'd shoot hundreds of shots and handle the ball for hours every day.) He was an absolute professional all the time; in fact years later when I purchased the team he was the one I called for consultation. After hours of talk and planning I was prepared to offer him the general manager's job.

In those days Hallie and I knew we were unbeatable. He and I talked about recruiting Oscar and Wilt and taking on the world's best teams when the tour was over. Neither of us drank or smoked, and our conditioning regimen kept us injury-free for a long while, so we were Abe's role models for the other players. However, as time went on, I found I was becoming less and less interested in pretending to be a basketball superstar indefinitely. By this point in my career I had completely validated the fact that I was a player of significance – later that year I led the team in scoring average during the all-star tour before damaging a knee – but I knew my game and I knew my game's limitations. Besides, my sights were now set on bigger accomplishments.

From the very moment I first spoke of my basketball ambition to Abe Saperstein at the age of 12, I unknowingly began writing my Harlem Globetrotters and sports dream script, which for now had all come to pass. I had a little celebrity and a brief but great global adventure. There had been competition, all-star games, travel, television, great friendships with Meadowlark, Hallie and others, and hundreds of hours of lessons learned from the game's master, Abe Saperstein. I now needed to write a new dream: I wanted very much to go to Harvard or Wharton (which I eventually did) to study business.

Luckily, I had money. I basically saved all of what I earned, and confirmed Albert Einstein's theory that the most amazing phenomenon in math is the effect of compound interest. It was time to think of moving on to the next phase of my life.

5 BUSINESS: MY NEW GAME

How is business like basketball? Rely on your teammates. Know what's expected of you. Ask questions regularly. Be honest, be on time, and be prepared. Give everything 100 percent hustle. These are rules I'd long lived by. So, not surprisingly, during my time with the Tuck Tapers, I had discovered I had an unusual business IQ and I could function with ease in the business world.

As I mentioned, the New York Tuck Tapers and the other Industrial League teams, unlike any other sports organizations, offered their professional athletes development opportunities. Fortunately, I had been among several players selected on my team to train in one of the business areas. The arrangement was explained to me like this: If the market was paying up to $1,000 a week for an accountant or sales representative, Tuck Tapers owner Paul Cohen would pay that market rate nine months per year. The other three months, he paid 50 percent of the base rate plus a full basketball salary based on the player's stature and output. That amount could theoretically be from $1,000 to $4,000 a week. If this worked as described, the salary represented big basketball money in those days (in fact, good minor league money today). My absolute dream goal was to make $100,000 a year: well above the NBA average, more than all but the biggest Globetrotter stars made and, by my calculations, 10 times teachers' pay. It was an amount many times more than my dad ever dreamed of earning.

During my Tapers tenure, I worked on the national customer service desk handling marketplace and product logistics from all over the country. Our products – mostly discounted bulk sales of pressure-sensitive tapes – competed with those of the Minnesota Mining and Manufacturing Company (3M). Customer contacts were usually by phone, and I possessed the voice and diction that prevented callers from identifying me as a Black person. (This was the original "don't ask, don't tell" charade I'd learned from my light-skinned relatives from Chicago.) All that call-in customers knew was that Mannie worked long hours and was adept at solving their problems.

The Tuck Tape Company was successful because of Paul Cohen's leadership, work ethic and responsiveness to customer concerns. His internal brand messages were simple: 1) *Price matters*; and 2) *Our product will work as promised or we will make it right*. He vowed, "We will be the manufacturing and price leader in the areas we serve." I liked the way he thought about his company and, in fact, I was successful to the point where I once taught a sales and service class based on Mr. Cohen's philosophy. In case you are wondering, I wasn't very good at it – but my boss loved my effort and how seriously I took the assignment.

I wanted to be a future Paul Cohen, so great was my admiration for this special man. By the time I knew him, he had late stage multiple sclerosis, and was physically handicapped but very sharp mentally. He was a genuinely good person and wanted to help people achieve their dreams. Imagine, even in those days he would always find and put the most qualified people on the big jobs. Color, age or gender didn't seem to matter. He placed college all-star basketball player and tennis ace

Worthy Patterson in a senior executive job, gave my teammate Jim Daniels and his older brother big jobs in finance and operations, and made my friend Ed Raiser the lead buyer for the company.

A brilliant operator and company spokesperson, Ed was a street-smart voice of logic and wise counsel. He once told me he had this part-time job and asked if I would help him out on a Saturday and Sunday. We met at the Westchester Country Club and he tells me to grab a bag and that we would be working a big-money match. Imagine my surprise: Ed was a big-time Black executive with a private office and personal secretary, and here he was a weekend golf caddy. He could afford to join the club. He told me two things: First, he hated the game of golf even though he was a genius as a caddy. And, second, he saved every penny for his kids' education. Even more passionately, he went on to tell me that he wanted to own his own procurement business in five years. What a great day we had. The gentlemen we worked for were bankers and they loved Ed and his stories. I was amazed at his knowledge and leadership. The four players scored great and gave us both very large tips and a bag full of food and drinks. My takeaway was this: Education and honest work are the best investment we make in our future, and that even my corporate idol had a bigger dream.

My affinity for business was solidified during my time with the Tuck Tapers and being involved with Mr. Cohen's company; I knew the business world was where I was eventually headed. During my stints with the Globetrotters, I was constantly sending resumes and interviewing, seeking either a position or inclusion in a management training program. Much of my energy in the years immediately thereafter was devoted to identifying a satisfactory entry point to bigger challenges. But finding the right challenge turned out to be an enormous hurdle of its own.

* * *

Even after I left the Globetrotters, job applicants were required to include a photo with each resume. One reason for this practice soon became apparent. Though I applied for positions at a variety of levels, I systematically received standard rejection form letters so impersonal that reading them made me feel like garbage. Most of my inquiries simply went unanswered. Years later, this seemed pretty ironic. I would be a future Honeywell president, a Fortune 500 board director, a National Science Fellow, a successful hard-driving entrepreneur and owner of the Harlem Globetrotters. But how could those human resource managers have guessed my potential if they never talked to me? I just wanted a chance, but the only thing they seemed to care about was that I was a Negro.

What I gradually discovered was that – other than a few small, Eastern companies like Tuck Tape – people of color were seldom (to put it mildly) found working at white-collar levels in American business. Most toiled in factories and at other labor-intensive positions. Back then, I met only one Black advertising executive – even though post-war African-Americans were buying cars, hair products, soft drinks, good whiskey, automobiles and automobile insurance to the tune of over $40 billion per year. How do you explain that? The advertising executive I met in Detroit was Doug Alligood of the firm BBD&O. Highly effective and brilliant, he moved around the office like Magic Johnson with a kick-ass attitude. One of his accounts was Pepsi Cola – and to this day, if given a choice, I always favor Pepsi.

During the basketball off-seasons, I tried my hand at a few other careers. I did some substitute teaching – enough to learn that this wasn't a final career choice for me. Teaching is hard work, and at inner city schools, teachers often felt close to disaster every day – or worse, they felt lost, tired and invisible. In Detroit and on Chicago's west side, the challenge was especially daunting. Not enough people seemed to care, and the few that did were underpaid, under-recognized and unappreciated.

The end of my teaching career came about out of personal frustration. One semester I took two of my classes to the Science Museum, and we all really enjoyed the great learning experience and the very knowledgeable guide who showed us around. I got approval to do it again the next month. This time I created a formal lesson plan and taught a two-hour class on "Energy and the Emerging Sciences" on-site. My eighth grade students were thrilled, and I asked them what their parents thought of our field trip, since I wanted parents to also take their families on a periodic basis. The room was silent for a long time. Then a loudmouth from the back of the room yelled out, "My dad said if you're so damned smart, why are you working in this nasty ass place?" I was hurt, but more than that, I was so glad it was Friday and I'd have a weekend to figure out the answer to the question and shake the feeling of failure.

The bell rang after a silence of at least 10 seconds. I said loudly to the class, "Our weekend assignment will be a one-page answer to that question, including my own. The best write-ups will get free lunch and tickets to the White Sox game. Class is dismissed. Have a good weekend." Fifteen minutes later I made my way to the principal's office and turned in my classroom keys. Most of the other male teachers had left 45 minutes earlier to race to their second jobs at the post office, so I picked up my paycheck, said half-hearted goodbyes to the few people around, and strolled to my car with thoughts of the weekend on Chicago's south side. I dreamed more than ever over the next two days of being rich and powerful enough to change the nation's education system. Teachers deserved better and our youth deserved better role models. Teaching was a laudable career, but something was definitely not right.

I had another brief career during that period as well. I never got hired by the U.S. Post Office, so I decided that a good way to make extra money – and meet women – was to work in retail. I eventually got hired by a discount shoe company on the near south side of Chicago to work two nights a week in one of its stores. Every hour on that job I'd ask, "What the hell am I doing here?" It was way too painful. I later sold vacuum cleaners door-to-door for nine months; and while I was setting sales records, my target customers were victims of their personal greed through a financing and rebate scheme, hours of loneliness (I was someone to talk to), and regrettably ignorance. The contracts were complicated and the actual product itself was great but far exceeded the needs of the clientele.

Now, post-Globetrotters, I couldn't get any traction in the job market. Something was wrong with this picture. I had a degree that was academically solid from a major university, had traveled the world, and had worked responsibly for Technical Tape (even though I couldn't muster up the nerve to call Mr. Cohen and ask about my old job, in part because of my ego and also because I didn't want to deal with starting over in New York).

I thought about the Armed Services. The special services guys from the Army had once offered me just about everything to join the military in a special publicity pre-game ceremony in Chicago Stadium. At that point, I was viewed as the perfect south side Chicago poster child for encouraging enlistments. In exchange, I'd play ball, travel and promote the military as a career and personal development option. It never seriously entered my mind to do anything like this, so I stalled and enjoyed the attention – often thinking, "Wouldn't the military be a great career option for young people if it actually worked this way for everyone?" I kept thinking about all the Hollywood war movies with no Black heroes, no Black leaders, and no Black actors who ever got the girls or celebrated at the end, and I kept thinking about my dad's experience. Dad said, "To hell with the military. They screwed one Jackson with their lies and prejudice, and that's enough."

During this period of personal uncertainty, I'd meet white ex-college classmates who were moving along up the ladder with major corporations. I began to understand there was a fence between me and the type of future I had envisioned as a teenager. My initial response was anger – deep anger. For the first time, I began taking a really hard look at hardcore civil rights movements and studying alternative forms of government. This one wasn't working for people like me. I found myself remembering those nice Eastern Europeans, and resenting the way their American counterparts responded to me in their stores and shops around the city. Here at home, all that seemed to matter was skin color. White people of all ethnic backgrounds – Irish, French, German, Polish, Italian and what have you – always seemed first in line at the hospitals, at the banks, and at the schools. People my color got nothing, or what was left over that no one else wanted. I loved all people, but the American socio-political system was all messed up. I wanted to focus on getting rich and powerful enough to change things, and to extend a genuine hand to people like me who were left behind.

Having been in the business world for a while, I had begun to understand financial power. No one cared that Paul Cohen was Jewish, or that he was handicapped. He could say what he believed and hire anyone he wanted. The same was true for Abe Saperstein, and for my Italian high school coach, Joe Lucco. Maybe people said things behind their backs, but they were still able to build their own futures. Other than Martin Luther King, Malcolm X, a few other rights advocates and a few marginalized entertainers and sports figures, whom could I point to in my race to emulate?

Jesse Jackson had been right all along. Education alone was neither the problem nor the solution. At age 23 I felt trapped, totally embarrassed and ashamed of my country and weary of promises not kept. Having already turned down the "ambassador" role in the Army, I was drifting. Although I was drafted and deferred conditionally (due to my basketball knees), the specter of not being drafted was already haunting me.

The scene around me was both confusing and terrifying, and I had no use for advice that boiled down to, "Keep you chin up." Black contemporaries were becoming underpaid coaches and teachers, postal workers, truck drivers or, too often, inmates. Black athletes who had not received degrees ignored their declining sports skills and attempted to hang on to flimsy minor league careers. Some were already falling over the edge of the middle class and back into street life. There was a lot of talk on the streets about hatred, Black separatism, Communism and race wars. I began to recall Howard Popham – the old golf pro from my hometown who told me I was lucky to earn a modest living doing odd jobs. Had he been right? Had I wasted my time, and my dreams?

I was determined not to panic. My family didn't know my fears, and remained supportive. They always said, "You'll find a way. You always do. There is plenty of time." I began taking graduate school courses. At the suggestion of a friend, and because of my science aptitude, which was discovered during testing at Illinois and subsequently at job fairs for two pharmaceutical companies, I tested for a government-funded National Science Fellowship and was accepted. The federal government had funded a nationwide sweep to find science talent in hopes of closing the growing Cold War technical gap between the U.S. and Russia. I was certain that if I was successful, this new credential would influence corporate thinking as to my potential and competence. But as just one example of that faulty logic, when I later answered an advertisement that offered entry-level management training with the Rexall Company in St. Louis, a venue where I felt I was known, I was tested, interviewed, then, after talking for hours rehashing basketball stories, shown the revolving door.

Lonely, I entered into a marriage to a nice, bright young woman that would last only a few difficult years. This too was a product of my fears and my search for stability. I craved and missed the pinnacle I once experienced in sports. I seemed to be working and studying harder and harder with too little to show for the effort. I had yet to learn the virtues of wisdom and patience.

I was facing life's realities, which I couldn't run from, or jump over. In basketball, you could shoot a ball 30 times, make 15 of those shots, and be a hero. In real life you couldn't succeed that way. Nor could you simply turn the page to the next game. Those transitional years were proving to be some of the most difficult of my life. Out of college, you discover you really are on your own. You also recognize that small missteps or a single bad move at this stage can influence your entire life. Every "shot" and every decision seemed to count, and a misstep stayed with you. Nobody had ever warned me how many landmines would be sprinkled around choices made in early adulthood.

Since leaving the shelter of Edwardsville, I had to quickly learn on my own how to assess risk and how to keep score in my new arena. Many friends and family assumed I had it all. They would ask why I lived so conservatively, and why I was so concerned about the future all the time. I was constantly being chided to loosen up. After all, by their standards I was living the African-American dream; I had youth, cash in the bank, new cars and a college degree. But, for the time being, this all seemed to be trumped by being born a person of color. I was losing valuable time and positive energy. Behind the doors of the jobs I held, life was a bitch and I had no one to talk to about it or to blame but myself. In many ways other than race, I wasn't prepared. Still, I counted my blessings. Genetics and fate had dealt me a strong hand, with my height, appearance, communication skills, stamina, social quotient and intellect. Something kept telling me good fortune would eventually come to my rescue. It turned out that despite my obstacles and anxieties, that remained my strongest and constant fundamental view of life.

* * *

Waiting for my big break, I moved to Detroit hoping to play semi-pro ball, hang around the Pistons organization, and be near the auto industry scene. I was warmly welcomed to the city by Earl Lloyd, a former teammate of Don Ohl. My college and high school teammate, Earl gave me a lot of positive encouragement and solid advice and opened his home to me for several weeks. I played pick-up games with first-round draft pick and All-Star Dave Bing (Syracuse rookie, future Hall of Famer, and future mayor of Detroit). Dave's unbelievable moves and skills helped me accept the fact that it would be okay for this 25-year-old to find a reason for leaving the game, which would happen soon enough.

The big breakthrough I'd been waiting on for four years came while I was working on a master's degree at the University of Detroit and practicing basketball from 9:00 to 11:00 each night. Strong Black-White relationships were rare at the time, but I developed a lifelong friendship with a fellow basketball player named John Watson. John, a

6-foot-7 University of Detroit team captain, was a solid ball player with great hands and a very respectable mid-range shot. We both enjoyed retelling the story of how in our first meeting, after shooting together one night, I challenged him to a sprint race on the court. He flat out beat me soundly on two occasions and would never race me again. The only excuse I had was my recent knee surgery. In truth, though, he was a very fast runner and an excellent wing player on the fast break. *

An economist and psychologist, Dr. John Watson, who worked for General Motors, was a unique and brilliant young man who would ultimately finish his career as dean of the Business College at St. Bonaventure University. As our young friendship began to grow, he and his equally brilliant wife, Sue, came to understand my anxieties related to career and race. Sensitive to the obstacles I was confronting, John eventually introduced me to his supervisor, Dr. Jim Oliver, a senior executive and vice president at General Motors Cadillac Division.

Dr. Oliver was the pre-eminent clinical psychologist at the Cadillac car division. He had devised a series of core predictive achievement tests for people seeking executive careers within General Motors, which was then one of the world's five largest and most successful publicly held corporations. These tests were heralded as predictors of success, and had been scientifically validated by GM's elite upper management teams. GM believed that corporate leaders had to be something like a minimum of 130 percent smarter (as indicated by test scores) than those they supervised. I never believed it then as I don't now; nevertheless, this was the benchmark I would be expected to meet.

I was warned that the tests were exhausting and extremely difficult. I didn't care. I was anxious to take them anyway. After informing me that my initial Wonderlic score of 38 was exceptional, Dr. Oliver asked me sternly and straight-up if I had cheated. Unconvinced by my denial, he proceeded with several more tests and eventually retested me with the Wonderlic. I scored a 46.

Dr. Oliver hired me to administer those same tests, and to oversee a company-wide apprenticeship program for skilled trade workers, new hires and internal executives. As he took me around to meet officers in the company, Dr. Oliver invariably would introduce me as, "Mannie Jackson, the young colored guy with the 46 Wonderlic and the 94th percentile in Adaptability, Guilford Zimmerman and Minnesota Paper Form Board."

The Adaptability Test evaluated reactions to various management scenarios; the Guilford Zimmerman Temperament Survey (GZTS) assessed personality traits related to organizational success; and the Minnesota Paper Form Board tested aptitudes related to success in mechanical and engineering occupations. Evidently, Dr. Oliver was fascinated and pleased with the fact that someone with my background could master his tests. I was not sure why he was surprised, as I knew full well how much my life to date had required adaptability, team skills and an expertise in spatial relationships (how else can you keep track of everything that is going on on a basketball court?).

Still, I knew Dr. Oliver was proud of me. Working with him and John Watson, both PhDs, I soon realized how limited my formal education had been and how hard I would have to work just to keep up. I did though, and Oliver tolerated all my inexperience and flaws along the way. I liked him and we got along really well. Yet while working in his department was a pleasure, and the GM job was my start, this part of corporate structure was an area that failed to hold my interest.

I wanted management and leadership responsibilities. I wanted to make a lot of money. I also wanted to make policy and change corporate America. I knew there were dozens of Black guys my equal or better who hadn't yet met their "Trojan Horse" in the form of a John Watson. After recruiting and administering aptitude tests for 18 months I could do it in my sleep, and would predict test results like it was a game. I found that if I could speak to an applicant for just 30 minutes, I was right about 70 percent of the time.

A case in point: While at GM, I invited a young boxer named Hedgeman Lewis to come in and test with us. I met him while attending amateur fights at Brewster Center in Detroit. (Detroit had the best fight clubs in the nation, and I wanted to learn to box. I also thought it would be interesting to one day market the fight business.) I encountered Hedgeman while hanging out with Ray Scott, Detroit Pistons coach and owner of a prominent fight club. After 30 minutes, my intuition prompted me to invite the up-and-coming fighter to come to GM and take Dr. Oliver's test.

Most of the boxers were hip, hardcore, street kids. Usually very mean and very skilled as fighters, they were actually easy to get to know. I soon recognized that several of these young guys were really intelligent. When Hedgeman showed up at the office, eyebrows were raised. But sure enough, I administered the test and struck gold. Hedgeman scored a 45-plus compared to Oliver's perfect 50 and my 46. The typical plant general foreman would score in the mid-30s. Hedgeman left the office after the test, but Dr. Oliver wanted to see him and talk to him. The young fighter's score had completely shattered Oliver's paradigm, and he wanted to know more. This was not to be, however. Six months later, Hedgeman resurfaced in Los Angeles, managed by actor Ryan O'Neal and fighting on national television for the Welterweight Championship of the world. How many more were out there like him? Oliver, Watson and I talked for hours one night about the country's wasted African-American assets.

On a personal level, I found myself inspired by Hedgeman – although less by his scores than by his belief in himself and his determination to lead and grow. He was single-minded about being a leader and a champion, and his example vaulted me back into my offensive mindset again. Soon after meeting him, I decided to explore the possibilities of owning a business, starting with a Cadillac dealership.

Meanwhile, I noticed a problem in the company's finance and administration area, dealing with education and training, which was costing GM millions of dollars. So after six months of research, I submitted a recommended procedure for change, which paid off to me personally in the form of hundreds of thousands of dollars. With this new-found wealth and life experiences, I was fired up again. I was in active dream mode, and knew my business career game was just beginning. No more doubt or fear. I, too, set my sights on being a champion.

Some months later, I found myself in Minneapolis as a representative of the automobile industry, to speak on one of General Motors' pet topics – white-collar unionism. No employer wants disgruntled office workers. When treated unfairly with regard to pay and personnel policies, employees either leave or seek a forum to voice their dissatisfaction. When a majority shared the same fears, their logical course was to seek powerful and experienced third-party representation. My purpose was to help management initiate a process of preventive care and predictive maintenance when dealing with employees in offices and factories.

With Dr. Oliver as a mentor, I was well-versed on my subject, and my presentation in Minneapolis went splendidly. In addition, during a Q & A session that followed, I mentioned my career aspirations and dreams of ultimately running my own business.

Afterward, an executive from Honeywell, Inc., which was based in Minneapolis, approached me and asked if I had any interest in relocating. It was just the breakthrough for which I'd been hoping.

---

*My friend, John Watson, passed suddenly and unexpectedly on April 17, 2011. This is an excerpt from a letter concerning this book, written by John on March 22, 2011:

I remember playing basketball at a local gym when Mannie came to play. They asked me to guard him. His first run down the court, he hit an 18-foot jumper; the next time, he dunked right over me.

At the time, I was working in the Cadillac division of GM. Mannie was looking for a job after working out with NBA teams. He was close to making the teams in both cities, but back then, the teams had quotas and only the top two or three made the teams. I told him he should come to my work to interview. He said they'd never hire a Black guy, and I told him the hiring was all based on tests. The next day, he came to GM and tested in my division and had one of the highest Wonderlic scores the administrator had ever seen. Mannie worked with me until we were both transferred to the Labor Relations Division. In the late 60s, during the Detroit riots, my wife and I lived nearby the action. We decided to leave for our Port Huron lake house. We invited Mannie and his family to join us. It was getting really dangerous, both in our neighborhood and at work. Mannie wouldn't go, due to looting and on principle. He said, "I am going to stay on my floor with a gun and shoot anyone that comes in."

When the riots were over, I was playing recreational ball with Mannie and his friend, Gov Vaughn. I was the only white guy in the gym and I really didn't want to go in. Mannie said I would be okay to go in because I was with him, and he was right. I actually got a standing ovation for going into that gym that day, thanks to Mannie.

MANNIE JACKSON

6 TWO HONEYMOONS

My encounter with members of the Honeywell team marked an amazing and gratifying new phase in my life. It was a phase in which I would be lucky enough to fall in love... twice. The first time was with a company and its culture; the second time was with the woman who would become my life partner. Before I met and married Cathy, however, I would embark on my Honeywell honeymoon.

General Motors provided the doorway to the corporate world, but the executives at Honeywell were the ones who ultimately offered general management experience and advancement opportunities in line with my entrepreneurial goals. Since the late 1800s, Honeywell had distinguished itself as a leader in automated controls for residential and commercial buildings, manufacturing, data processing, aviation and defense. At the time I joined the company, the Honeywell brand had a pervasive presence. When it came to name recognition and respect, it had the same impact as great brands we think of today as iconic: Coca Cola, Pepsi, Apple, McDonalds. Honeywell's most widely known product was undoubtedly the "Round." This distinctive little thermostat was found in more homes and commercial buildings than almost any other product in the world, and came to symbolize the Honeywell brand.

For me, Honeywell was a case of "love at first sight." The company had good intentions, solid values and a core of integrity. I knew then, as I know now, that whatever success I had or would have in the future I would owe in part to that business culture and the foundation it provided me.

Honeywell was located in Minneapolis, Minnesota, one of the most beautiful and livable cities in the world. When I moved to Minnesota, I went into immediate culture shock. In Detroit, I'd been immersed in Black struggles, empowerment movements and adjustments to life in the aftermath of the city's 1967 race riots. (In the summer of '67, a police raid on an after-hours "Blind Pig" bar precipitated a series of confrontations that resulted in 43 dead, nearly 500 injured and over 2,000 buildings destroyed. My friends and I, at a late-night party two blocks away at the home of Pistons power forward Ray Scott, heard the noise and thought little of it at first.) In Minneapolis, being greeted by smiling white men and women felt strange at first. Even more startling was seeing the happy – albeit relatively few – persons of color on the streets. I remember joking about my surroundings at the time, and wondering how I had landed on this planet. I had become so jaded by riots and race problems, that I initially greeted welcoming gestures and events with a heavy dose of cynicism and distrust.

Unfortunately, the scarcity of Blacks in the streets was a phenomenon repeated in the hallways of big business. I remember thinking that the inside of corporate America looked a little like the NBA had 10 years earlier. I wondered for a moment if there wasn't a similar quota system. Or maybe the corporate management world just decided it was going to be white, because this was likely the way God had intended it. At this point in my life, I was well aware that things could be so different. I was no longer the provincial 21-year-old leaving Illinois. I had already traveled to over 70 countries. I'd also worked for

Paul Cohen in New York, and seen firsthand the power of a diverse workforce. I knew this country had countless thousands of underutilized minority and female professionals who were ready, willing and very able to make this country stronger and better.

I was frustrated, but overall I'd think, "It's my time now, and I've got something to prove so that others will fill the pipeline and have it easier." I knew it was time for me to figure out how I could score and win. My attitude was, as always, *I will do whatever it takes*. I knew I was prepared to learn, thanks to all the great teachers I'd had in my past, from Alma Aitch and Ms. Moomaw to Joe Lucco, Paul Cohen, Abe Saperstein, John Watson and Jim Oliver. By now my life's journey had seen the best and the worse of just about everything, and I thought I no longer had to deal with my own doubts and fears of unworthiness. My dreams were legitimate and my skills were starting to become laser-focused. I made a conscious decision that any residual bitterness from the riots would remain in the background.

For that matter, so would my sports history. I wanted a fresh start and the opportunity to be judged solely on my abilities and contributions as a business player. (I was so successful at hiding my sports background that years later, when I became the out-front person in an ownership group that was trying to place an NBA franchise in San Diego, my former involvement with athletics became a media focus, and many of my Honeywell colleagues were stunned. It's amazing how differently information moved, or did not move, before the days of the Internet.)

I was learning the language of the business world and I was building a track record of bringing measurable value. Somehow I knew I had the toughness, make-up and resilience to overcome all the obstacles and nonsense. More importantly, I loved business as a way of life, the way

I had loved basketball years earlier. However, the references I had to winning came from the boxcar in Illmo, Missouri (the boxcar metaphor was to become my mantra), the locker rooms in Europe, the Big Ten, and schoolyard outdoor basketball courts in just about every city and under every imaginable condition. In all those situations you stayed up and in the game by winning, not bitching. I decided to approach business as "the big game," remembering all the lessons learned, especially from the boxcar, streets life and from basketball. I felt business was going to be my way not only of getting very wealthy and of gaining the means to be philanthropic, but also of helping to bring about much-needed change.

* * *

As symbiotic as my union with Honeywell would turn out to be, my initial experiences were frustrating. Despite assurances, I was given a nice but disappointing assignment in human resources. Although it came with the title of director, it proved to be less demanding than my former position with GM's Cadillac Motor Car Division. In fact, I sometimes felt it essentially involved supplying proof to government investigators that the company was in compliance with federal equal opportunity mandates. (As I gained more experience over the years, it became clearer how strategically critical these human resource jobs are in top-tier companies.) I knew that behind my back some of my cohorts labeled me "just another affirmative action character." I felt they badly underestimated the potential of people who looked like me, and I was tired of being underestimated.

Ultimately, many of these skeptics would end up working for me as I moved from human resources to marketing to factory management, became a vice president and general manager and, finally, became the corporation's worldwide corporate administration and marketing officer. In my final position, I sat beside CEO Mike Bonsignore, a good man who respected my opinions, gave me freedom and watched my back as I did his. Along the way I would learn from Fran Miller, Bob Rose, Bill Wray, Bill George, Kyle Carpenter and Chairman Ed Spencer important lessons of lasting value. But before all that happened, my life took a couple of detours.

The first detour was one I initiated. Impatient and disappointed with my undemanding Honeywell jobs, I again called on my old friend, Hall of Famer Earl Lloyd. He agreed to connect me with a new Chrysler program – one that prepared qualified minority candidates to become dealership owners. My new fired-up attitude and stature had me confident and ready to take a risk, and it was no secret that I loved cars and the car business. Chrysler accepted me immediately. I returned to Detroit and made a down payment on a beautiful two-story home in one of those exclusive neighborhoods that upper class whites literally abandoned following the riots. This place had everything one expected to see in a Hollywood estate. But within five days I learned that my business situation, while well intentioned, was not what I had been led to believe.

This was an era of great economic flux in the inner cities, and my role was initially shaping up to be manager of minority franchises – the point person responsible for shutting down minority dealerships that were failing. Do this, I was told, and when the economic wheel turned up again, I'd be in line for my own dealership. On the flip side, it turned out that minority dealerships were being offered mainly in areas that white owners were evacuating: areas where credit was poor and the chance of success minimal. Maybe I should have viewed this as an advantage to be exploited, but I didn't fully appreciate the situation. Besides, some soul searching revealed that deep down I wanted one day to be chairman of a major company. I had gotten too close not to recognize the scale of social change and the ability to correct the glaring imbalances in wealth and opportunity that it would be possible to execute from that platform. The good news was that Earl Lloyd understood, and he supported my decision to leave this enterprise behind. (It would take another book to delve into details regarding Earl Lloyd's friendship and inspiration, and what his mentoring and storytelling meant to my career and to hundreds of others.)

Meanwhile, Honeywell had been calling. This time it was the vice chairman, who set forth a guarantee of executive training and advancement. There were eight businesses operating under the Honeywell holding company structure then, and up-and-coming executives would have opportunities to live either in the progressive Minneapolis community or wherever in the world their careers developed. (I didn't know it at the time, but Honeywell and General Electric were in the closing stages of Honeywell acquiring GE's computer interests and my name had come up as part of the transition team.) Honeywell sent a plane ticket, and I immediately flew back to a union that would prove to be as challenging as it was rewarding.

But I mentioned there would be two detours in my early years at this company. The first, my car dealership foray, was my idea. The second was anything but. My progress was put on hold by a life-threatening development.

* * *

I was spending what I thought would be a fun Labor Day weekend in St. Louis with family and friends when my life got derailed. During a professional basketball game years earlier, I was accidentally kicked in the side while down on the floor. My injuries, which I thought to be only broken ribs, actually included a badly bruised diaphragm. Ten year later, during that fateful weekend, my diaphragm ruptured, spilling bile and other waste into my chest cavity.

I saw a succession of doctors and visited numerous hospitals before one esophageal and three chest surgeries, along with antibiotics, was determined to be the right course of action. What a nightmare and wake-up call. All my work, all my preparation – only for my well-conditioned body to put me on the sidelines. It was as if my light switch was suddenly shut off.

I spent two months in intensive care. The infection was extreme, and the amount of bile and fluids drained from my body was so prodigious that even the hospital staff and visiting medical experts were baffled. I lay in my small hospital bed just half awake, feeling like the incredible shrinking man. I was down from 185 pounds to less than 100.

I would think over and over, "I'm not ready to give up this life. My career is just getting started and I've got too much yet to achieve." I'd wake up every night at 2:00 or 3:00 a.m. thinking about every game of basketball I'd played, every class I wished I'd paid better attention in, and all the subjects and people I wanted to know more about. I wasn't even 30 years old. I was being told by every one to keep the faith, stay positive and not give up.

Typically, at 3:00 to 4:00 a.m. the nurses would come in with medication and we'd talk. Without fail, I would get sad, and then start weeping quietly before falling asleep. Every night seemed to be the same. Except for one night, which I think of as my "my blue light night." On this night, I became severely ill and it felt to me that I had died. At one point I thought I was drifting into the afterlife. I looked down from the ceiling and saw myself curled up on the small ICU bed, swathed in blue light. Several things occurred and were said in that room that night that the staff said I should not have known about, since I was lying there heavily medicated and semi-conscious – yet I had been aware of them. As time has passed, I'm remembering less and less about this near-death experience, but I know it happened.

At another point, I was so far gone that a rumor spread that I had actually died. Yet somehow I pulled through. Although it took months before the right corrective medical measures were finally implemented, I had an incredible amount of other kinds of support.

My mom and dad would visit daily to bring reassurances and love from friends and neighbors. My sister Marjorie came in from her home in Chicago every week with stories about the windy city. Friends would show up from every phase of my life to recount memories and tell stories. So many people showed up that I was eventually assigned a large private room; a big change from the original eight-bed ward of dying patients.

Little did I know at the time how much this event, while not taking my life, would forever change it. I had many revelations during this episode. For one thing, any lingering thought of playing competitive basketball was completely erased. More importantly, I would never again question how much the love of family and friends meant. It occurred to me very profoundly how essential supportive relationships are to our existence.

Most important of all, even when I was most crippled in mind and body, I found I still had hope and the power of God-given determination. Lying in bed, I ultimately discovered a very comfortable spiritual place that I continue to inhabit today. I saw how blessed my life had been and I felt so much gratitude for the hundreds of people who had helped me along the way. I also became determined to navigate around barriers and obstacles that I had come, at times, to use as excuses.

Once I left the hospital, I knew more had changed about me than my body type. In a real sense, I was reborn. Still, I needed to convalesce. I went to my parents' home. When I got there I had no strength in my once-powerful arms and legs. Mom soon took care of that with a regimen of five meals a day – supplemented by neighbors bringing milkshakes, cakes and pies over on a daily basis.

Six more months elapsed before I would return to Minneapolis. At first, I was shaken and afraid; the world and everything around me seemed dangerous and intimidating. But I had made up my mind not to ever feel sorry for myself as I was determined to return to normal. In fact, I never went back for the doctor-prescribed follow-up visits, but rather put myself through a modified "boot camp." The results were amazing to me, and to others, as I moved into a mode of challenging everything and everybody.

One day at a summer cookout, a family friend, Jerry Moulton, who had driven from Minneapolis to St. Louis with his wife Nancy to see me several times when I was ill, joked that he could now "have his way with me" in basketball. Twenty minutes later, we were going head to head – playing hard and trash talking. That went on for two hours. After going one-on-one, we went three-on-three with some others. When it was over, I looked at my Scandinavian buddy and, in between gasps for air, said as sincerely as I could "Thank you, old friend."

* * *

Back at Honeywell, things began to improve for me. That's not to say mine was as precise a path of development as had been promised. Several times supervisors found reasons to waylay me for a while, but I was both patient and persistent and had assurances that future evaluations would be based strictly on performance. Overall, each step at Honeywell was now viewed as a greater learning platform. My name had been placed on an executive development list to be fast-tracked for future corporate leadership.

Of course there were inevitable, if occasional, reminders that the world was still not all "under one roof" when it came to racial matters. At one point, a talented management employee resigned because he didn't want to work for a person of color. I had to go to my boss and say, "We just lost one of our best people because of me."

Even more devastating was a moment involving a top senior assistant who, I thought, had become a close friend. I was at his home for a festive holiday dinner when one of his sons said, "I'm so glad that a nice man like Mr. Jackson works for my dad." As the reality of the comment sunk in, I was crushed with disbelief. Momentarily, I felt like I was suffocating. It turned out that that for two years this man had been so embarrassed by the nature of our work association that he couldn't reveal to his family that I was his boss. He was a good man overall. He apologized and I forgave him over another dinner with his family. We moved on, both because I consider that kind of relentless, insidious bias a disease that should be pitied rather than punished, and because I was also developing a Teflon exterior to racial insults. I simply did not have time to nurse feelings of being insulted; I realized it was more useful to focus my energy on achieving results and protecting others.

Several very productive years passed. I had learned the lesson of developing "Saturday morning" relationships with literally hundreds of employees of all backgrounds and the nurturing advocates from all around the Honeywell world. My understanding of virtually every aspect of the company's many businesses expanded exponentially. My friendships with upper management grew strong, in part because I had hired, grown up alongside, and socialized with many of the company's most senior line executives and their families. In some cases I well knew I was a real live social experience; not only did I exploit it I would strive for sincerity and lasting friendships of trust by giving the extra mile and in my own case practicing the tolerance I had been preaching. And whether it was through tennis, golf, hunting, fishing or volunteer work, I always got involved and I was as close as one could get to feeling and understanding the pulse and temperature of corporate life and the language of survival in this sometimes strange corporate jungle. In order to win, I needed to know the rules and how this game was played both publicly and privately. And along the way I had to become the consummate insider.

I had many wonderful mentors during those years, and I not only benefitted from their counsel, but also observed them carefully. I remembered Coach Lucco's lessons on being a champion, which he believed starts by thinking and walking like a champion. So I began to study every move and gesture of corporate leaders. I observed how they dressed and how they spoke, and I even second-guessed their handling of crises to see what I'd do when and if my time came. I also came to understand the importance of trust, building relationships and managing confrontations.

Along the way I also learned to be a strong and confident writer. And my public speaking skills grew as well. Ironically, I also learned after the fact that when the decision had been made to offer me a senior executive position at Honeywell, the vice chairman had commented,

"Mr. Jackson has a serious speech and communication problem." Several advocates of mine reminded him that wasn't at all true and that I was, in fact, a popular and in-demand public speaker, as well as one of the founders and Chairman of the Executive Leadership Council. One person in the room said I had spoken at his church; another reminded him that I had spoken convincingly at one of Honeywell's very large customer's annual international sales meetings. The chairman relented on the spot, but to save face still insisted I take speech lessons from a theater group in Chanhassen, Minnesota. The head of that group became one of my best friends, and we'd laugh over lunch at my being there and how I refused to quit the so-called lessons because their group needed the money.

Soon thereafter, I was asked to join the transition team for Honeywell's GE computer acquisition. I was flattered and enthusiastic. I loved the energy, the learning and the emerging opportunities that grew from integrating two incredible cultures, listening to and commenting on acquisition issues and plans, participating in discussions around synergy, and being on a team I believed in. This experience really set the stage for my future skill set when it came to turning businesses around and managing the critical aftermath of buying and selling companies.

I was routinely the last person to leave the building in those days because I wanted to talk, listen, and learn. Invariably someone would come up to me at 8:00 or 9:00 p.m. and start to bounce marketing ideas my way or seek my help in conflict resolution. I would pay close attention to everyone who stopped in and take notes. My listening moments outnumbered teaching moments by 10 to 1, and the better listener I became the more my opinion was valued. Those times were exciting for all of us involved. In the Boston corridor alone there seemed to be new competitors every three or four months and technological innovation announcements weekly. The company found itself swirling in a beehive of constant spin-offs and start-ups. We were like a gang of young commandos or pioneers, because there was no precedent for so much information and technology being shared instantaneously by so many. We held the shareholders' dice for some of the highest stakes in corporate America and "accountability" was the mantra of every executive. Our leadership, led by Richard Douglas who in a strange way looked out for me and at every opportunity pushed my significance as a leader; was smart and strong, and there was no question: Only the strongest would survive; and my career, my confidence, my knowledge, and my net worth were suddenly being launched like a rocket

My instinct for the sciences gave me a third eye into the technical world of Honeywell, and the brief time I'd spent at Wharton helped me understand the questions raised by P&Ls, balance sheets, cash flow statements and the all-important returns on capital deployed. But as a colleague said to me one evening, this massive, complex endeavor was like turning first graders into MIT graduates overnight.

In later assignments, I continued my globetrotting, albeit minus my basketball. My travels carried me around the world: to Asia, where I spent one year negotiating for new telecommunication partners; to Stockholm, where I discussed software codes for systems integration with LM Ericsson; and to South Africa, where I gained management oversight and responsibility for future business in that nation through our subsidiary Martech Controls.

I would return to Minneapolis in between my travels, and at one point purchased a new home in Golden Valley, Minnesota. I searched for the perfect corporate-looking estate, and even allowed myself to engage in "one day" thoughts and dreams of being president or maybe even chairman of Honeywell. Only 25 years earlier I was a raggedy child sleeping on the floor of a railroad boxcar. Now I was in charge and responsible for things that mattered. I was an important stakeholder, or so I would keep telling myself, of a $12 billion Fortune 100 company with 100,000 employees in over 70 countries, and seriously thinking about leading this company from its stately mahogany paneled boardroom... "one day."

My dreams and ambitions grew bigger, the closer I got to the top. Perhaps I was beginning to border on delusional, but I needed a large target and the adrenalin it generated to keep my engine running at full speed. How else could I justify 16 trips to Europe and Africa in one year, or boarding a flight to Hong Kong on Christmas Eve? Big dreams can be big motivators. After all, the Chicago Cubs started every season hoping for a World Series ring, and I never once believed that Red Klotz didn't crave just one victory over the Harlem Globetrotters in Madison Square Garden or even Hibbing, Minnesota. In my case, the dream was a seat at the head of the table in the boardroom, and the ability to help every community charity committed to helping the poor and the struggling.

Fortunately, I had also found someone very special with whom I could share my corporate trophies.

* * *

In June 1974, I was returning from my Honeywell assignment in Tampa, Florida when I met my wife-to-be, Catherine P. Roberts. She was in Minneapolis to interview for a flight attendant's position with Northwest Airlines (this was before she received an MBA from Suffolk University). While awaiting the airport shuttle bus in the lobby of the Normandy Hotel, we shared a long and sometimes confrontational discussion about everything from race relations and affirmative action to marketing, economics and business planning. Mixed with these diverse topics were my assessments of Minnesota as a wonderful place to live and work.

Cathy was attractive, very bright and down to earth. I'd rarely met anyone who had a photographic memory like hers, and being with a person with that kind of recall was magical. (I was told that Ohio State All-Star Jerry Lucas had memorized the New York City phone directory while he played for the Knicks. I asked him one night if he could teach me, but I guess this ability is a genetic predisposition. To this day I've met only a few people with skills like his and Cathy's.)

I'd had platonic friendships with a number of women in the previous five years, and that same kind of friendship quickly developed between Cathy and me. In fact, I credit her with teaching me how to ski over the phone.

Later, as our friendship deepened, we addressed the fact that I was African-American and she was white. We didn't spend a lot of time sorting it out, but we knew there would be strong family reactions when I asked her to marry me. My family and her father were a little concerned, but very supportive from the start. Her mother, God rest her soul, was overwhelmed (as in *"What do we tell our friends?"* and *"What will they think of us?"* and *"What if you have children?"*) These reactions hurt, as it did when she quizzed everyone with the question, "What did we do wrong, for crying out loud?" Over the years, believe it or not, my mother-on-law and I became best of friends and I do miss her.

My view was that racial differences are too often overrated in relationships between individuals. To begin with, the odds of finding any person with whom you sincerely believe you will be compatible with for 40 or more years is fairly low. But Cathy and I started as friends, and knew how to treat one another respectfully. We also have similar interests, besides our love for each other and our families.

I was less concerned about family reactions than those of Honeywell's leadership. Bob Rose, the company's President of Field Engineering, and his wife Alice quickly put any concerns to rest, though, by hosting a wedding night dinner party at their New Hampshire compound. When this story got around the company, the combination of humor, surprise and romantic tales made for positive water cooler talk.

Cathy, all agreed, was an ideal corporate wife. She immediately got along with Ed and Harriet Spencer, which helped immensely. And if any customers or co-workers raised their eyebrows a bit when first seeing us together, I never noticed. In any case, they were soon speaking enthusiastically about the intelligent, well-focused young lady married to Mannie Jackson. Cathy makes friends easily, and her demeanor attracts confidence and loyalty. She had the capacity to truly trust and embrace everyone and never forget the smallest details of their lives; birthdays and children's names were simple, as were schools attended and clothing sizes. She would do all of this with pure intentions and sincerity. Much of my corporate success can probably be linked to an ability to make good choices about the people with whom I've surrounded myself, and the most important choice was my wife. She also embraced my 5-year-old adopted son Randall with kindness and love, and I knew we would build our own family one day.

To me, the most bonding aspect of any marriage is a decision to have children. In 1979 and 1981, we were blessed with two wonderful daughters, Candace and Cassandra, who have made us about as happy as two people can be. Since birth, they have existed in a socially integrated world. They have many friends who reflect both sides of their heritage. My personal goal assures both daughters the best and most comprehensive education possible at whatever cost. As it turned out, they were excellent students and graduated from top-tier colleges and graduate schools – NYU, DePaul and Columbia University. My oldest daughter, recently married, is thriving as a writer for the *Wall Street Journal* in New York City, and my youngest daughter, Cassandra, is exercising her marketing and sales skills in the vegan industry. Both are independent and happy. They have good health and great minds, and friends of all colors and backgrounds.

Cathy and I long ago agreed to be open and candid about the racial aspect of our children's lives. We stressed the positives of both sets of grandparents, and attempted to give the girls reasons to be proud of both their backgrounds. When pressed about their racial identity, they are comfortable with term "mixed race," and proud of our African-American lineage. We are all comfortable accepting that they are unique – neither Black, nor White, but a good blend of both.

In addition to sharing the joys and challenges of parenting, Cathy and I always had shared values. Out of survival and necessity, I have always been able to push through most obstacles and continue forward. I think my willingness to do so helped me navigate my way through a nearly all-white business world, and maybe helped in some small way to alter the culture of corporate America. With my enthusiastic wife and two daughters supporting me, my home team got stronger, and my abilities multiplied.

* * *

Another thing that has always been very important to Cathy and I is philanthropy. The act of giving helps us to remain happy, productive and positive. Cathy and I are both socially and politically active, and over time we have been blessed to be able to give millions of dollars to our favorite charities from health care, to education, and museums in Rwanda, Cape Town, New York City, Billings and St Louis. But to continue this level of giving, I had to do some additional earning. Fortunately, I made several successful investments outside of Honeywell.

As I advanced in the corporation to a salary and benefits situation that made our lives more than comfortable, I was also investing and making entrepreneurial moves designed to increase my future income potential. It was clear to me that the executive corporate retirement plan, social security and 401Ks wouldn't satisfy the needs of my family after we left the corporate world. Nor would these means alone allow us to participate in large-scale philanthropy.

I wanted to give of my time and expertise so that others like me would have a chance to realize their own dreams. With Jim Kaiser of Corning, Eleanor Williams of Sarah Lee, Al Martins of Xerox, Buddy James, and a few others, I helped found the Executive Leadership Council. Our goals were simple: support high-potential Blacks in all corporations, because doing so made excellent business sense. We set out to identify and support future leaders of global enterprises who happened to be Black, and to get as many African-Americans as possible involved in emerging economies, owning their own companies, and sitting on the boards of directors of Fortune 500 organizations. We vowed to be relentless, ethical and laser-focused – not as a civil rights organization, but as an organization of first-generation Black executives devoted to helping our companies become better world citizens and other African-Americans gain access to corporate chambers. Our belief was simple: that the pursuit of success, wealth and shared power on the part of all Americans was good for the world and our country.

It's often unfamiliarity with minority men (and virtually all women) that, as much as intolerance, causes any job candidate to have his or her career stalled. I remember my own experience of being assigned to a theater speech consultant, knowing I too would have been passed over without friends and advocates in the room. I've been a party to several debates where stumbling blocks to hiring occurred and where a committee reached consensus based on the lack of a strong advocate for a strong candidate. The Executive Leadership Council seeks to mitigate this problem. Today this organization has over 500 members, comprised of the most senior African-American corporate executives in Fortune 500 companies, representing well over 380 major corporations.

* * *

While at Honeywell, another event occurred that expanded my view about tolerance and intolerance – this time halfway around the globe. In 1990, I tried to get my Executive Leadership Council membership to stand up and publicly fight for a democratic South Africa. Only a few – Eleanor Williams, Jim Kaiser, Al Martins, Buddy James, Hazel O'Leary and Ann Fudge among them – wanted to take the "risk." Africa was a charged subject for many African Americans. The truth was that even I, as intellectually and emotionally committed as I was to this cause, had to admit that I did not know much about the real Africa. Like many Black Americans back in the day, my first images of Africa were drawn from the stereotypes of old Tarzan movies, actually believing that there was a continent of simple-minded natives that would allow an uneducated white man in a loin cloth to frighten and dominate them in their own environment while giving more comfort and respect to a damn monkey.

The image changed for me when I met proud African students at the university and later was given the opportunity to first visit the continent of Africa as a Harlem Globetrotter; and much later, the country of South Africa to explore new business possibilities for Honeywell Corporation. One visit to South Africa was enough to put a face on the country, the people and the problems. Two things shocked me. First was the incredible beauty of the land. Visually, it is one of the planet's jewels. The other was the shocking reality of what one group of human beings had done to another.

I walked through a corporate headquarters as sophisticated as any you would ever see in the United States and observed that the wealth of the ruling cartels was enormous. In one office, the art on the walls alone was worth a fortune. Despite widespread poverty, only a little research was required to learn there was more than enough land, food and natural resources for everyone to have an adequate share. I'm not talking socialism; I'm talking a fair shot in a free market. The colonists changed the culture and the rules of the economy to fit their version and standards so that they always won. (As my dad used to say, "He who has the gold, makes the rules.")

Later, we drove into a Black township and saw the shacks that passed for homes. The conditions made our worst ghettos in the United States appear princely by comparison. Hovels, measuring 12-by-12 feet and smaller, sheltered as many as a dozen people. What passed for furniture was whatever old hotels or even the poorest whites had thrown away. Heat from coal stoves gave off deadly fumes that would make your eyes burn. Leaving those homes in the evening, I'd walk bent over to avoid the layer of smoke that would form a low-lying umbrella over the villages of Alexander and Soweto.

I found myself thinking of the bombing of Hiroshima and the devastation in Korea and Vietnam. These apocalyptic events could not have been any more destructive than the apartheid affecting these innocent and sensitive people in their homeland. The longer I stared at this situation, the larger my eyes grew. Inwardly, I realized that some of what I was witnessing seemed familiar. Too much of what I witnessed looked and felt like my past life in my own country. So much reminded me of Illmo, Missouri, East St. Louis, Gary, Indiana, and hundreds of educationally deprived, racially divided and poverty-stricken townships and communities across America.

In my opinion, the process of dismantling apartheid was not just a moral imperative, but also an economic survival decision for the strongest region in sub-Saharan Africa. The white cartel leaders had to know that if they did not support a new order in which all people could participate, there would be a total collapse of the social order and, by extension, the overall economy. Fortunately, by this time Nelson Mandela had emerged from prison and was becoming the leading force behind a new political order. Black leaders from Coca-Cola, Pepsi and Apple Computers were already in the country and were making a difference. And other companies, including Xerox, Sara Lee and Corning, which had divested themselves of South African interests, began consulting with the African National Congress (ANC) about timetables for returning to the country.

I came to know Mandela, spent much time with him and his staff, and became an advocate for the ANC in the United States. Most of us were able to persuade our companies not to reinvest until signaled by the ANC and until free elections had been mandated. Honeywell subsequently operated two start-ups in the region. Later, Honeywell divested its majority interest in Martech Control and I became its board chairman and protector of its transition and investment interest. It was a pressure-packed experience that I cherished. Fortunately, Honeywell's resident senior manager was an excellent executive and very highly respected by all levels of employees, Black and White.

My role called for many return journeys to South Africa, and during 1994, my then 14-year-old daughter, Candace, accompanied me on one of them. Candace had been raised in a comfortable and integrated atmosphere in Minneapolis. When I'd tell her or her sister how it was in Harlem, South Central L.A., Gary, Indiana, or Southern Illinois during the 1950s and '60s, the stories were abstract to them. (When they saw an area where I once lived on the near south side of Chicago, their reaction was a blunt "This place looks awful! Why didn't you just move?") Now Candace was about to have her world view shaken.

Candace's previous impressions of South Africa had been television clips of fighting, terror and constant chaos. Before we left home, she wanted to know if we needed guards or would have to carry a gun. Once we were in South Africa, though, its initial impact on Candace was similar to what it had been on me. She looked out of a 20th-floor hotel window to see the beauty of Johannesburg's skyline. We went to a Sun City resort, attended a play, ate at a four-star restaurant, visited a game reserve and walked the beaches of beautiful Cape Town and Durban. "This is a neat place," she commented. "It must be nice to be wealthy and white here." Later, we drove to Soweto. We passed through the beautiful clean suburban white district, and then... what a shock! The next morning we visited a new squatter camp where people lived in conditions unimaginable to Candace. Candy met the people and saw that no matter how disadvantaged they were, the residents greeted one another cheerfully and laughed, played and worked together as families and a community. She soon discovered that their most valued asset was that, like her, they all dreamed of a better tomorrow.

While I was negotiating in the home of a white contractor who was interested in doing more business with Martech, Candace, in another room, struck up a friendship with his daughter. During an ensuing conversation, I pointed out that had we lived in South Africa, I could not have worked for a corporation like Honeywell as a business unit manager, that she and her new friend could not have lived in the same housing area, and that we might have had to live in a squatter's camp like the one she had seen. Candace greeted this reality first with disbelief and later with indignation, protesting, "They have no right to do that." I heard myself responding, "This will all have to change one day. With technological advancements in communications, with TV and the Internet, and with the growing numbers of righteous people both Black and White dreaming of a new order and a new reality, there will be another kind of future for this country." I also told her that one of these dreamers and leaders was a friend of her mother's and mine. "He's a smart, strong Black leader who cares about the well-being of all people. We'll meet him at the first Parliament meeting of the newly elected ANC in a couple days. His name you know well as Nelson Mandela, but as he is our friend you will call him *Madiba* (father)."

Candace did meet Mandela as we were among the first Blacks to order lunch and dine in the private parliament dining room. She and I then attended an elaborate celebratory dinner after the Parliament session. She had a magnificent and memorable experience as we all sat around a massive, ornate mahogany table talking with our friend Lindewe Mambuza, a charming Chief of Staff and later ambassador to Germany. We ate and we toasted everyone as we celebrated the new government and free elections. However, at around midnight I learned that one of the Zulu tribal chiefs desired my daughter's hand in marriage. I was first amused, and then shocked as I realized this could be serious stuff. I immediately excused myself and took Candace by the hand. We went to the door and began the two-mile walk back to our hotel laughing and recounting various versions of the story all the way. Around 3:00 a.m., I laid my head on the pillow and thought, what a day and what an unforgettable experience. My daughter was safe, happy and seemingly oblivious to all the possibilities that a father has to worry about.

* * *

Eventually, I became one of Honeywell's six top officers and one of eight on its corporate policy committee, as well as president and general manager of two successful ventures. But another highly successful endeavor was beginning to redefine my life's trajectory. I remember the tipping point incident in South Carolina at a combination Honeywell board and staff meeting announcing a major corporate restructuring. The night of the opening dinner for that event, Robin Leach featured my family on his *Lifestyles of The Rich and Famous* TV show. Most of the 30 or so spouses not attending the business meetings had watched the show. That evening as we entered the ballroom for dinner, Cathy whispered in my ear, "This feels awkward. Maybe it's time we consider leaving Honeywell."

I was not unhappy. My social achievements were noteworthy, my stature and reputation were solid. I was a millionaire several times over, and I was still young. But even at this stage I dreamed of more. I wanted to be more significant as a leader and role model, and free of the day-to-day internal politics and racial issues of major corporations.

Ultimately I stepped aside, closing the long and happy Honeywell chapter in my life. And like most important decisions, this one was based on many overlapping reasons. For one, it had become obvious that the final step up the Fortune 500 corporate ladder in my company would not be available to me. Chairman Mike Bonsignore respected me and I respected him, yet I don't feel he ever saw me for what I was eventually to become. He didn't see me going as far as he had. Who can blame him? Who would ever dream or guess that my background would result in a pioneering career that my dad referred to with pride as "an improbable long shot"? Who would have believed that a Black, all-star basketball player from the 1950s and '60s who once thought every game was an opportunity for him to score points would learn so completely to embrace the concepts of teamwork and collaboration?

In the early 1990's my San Diego friend Richard Esquinas enjoyed a brief, but stunning spin through the national media with his book entitled Michael and Me – detailing a series of golf matches with then NBA superstar, Michael Jordan.

I can't authenticate Esquinas' material but I do know that they played friendly games for high stakes. I played in a few of those games, which quickly got too pressure-packed for my "weekend" game and handicap. I have to say however, that I have never had as much fun or enjoyed playing the game with anybody before or since. As I remember, Jordan was a super competitor and Esquinas' game kept getting stronger and stronger. As his partner we seldom lost because of his calm short game and putting. Jordan was a master at getting into a competitors head. Honeywell, business travel and age were like anchors on my golf game as I could only compete with the two of them in spurts.

A pioneer in computer research, Harry Cooper, the uncle of Richard's wife, Kerry made a fortune from real estate gains and a company he'd sold years earlier. Prior to Richard's marriage to Kerry, he became as associate in one of Cooper's San Diego companies.

Cooper was a genius with a charismatic personality. His interest in sports was, at best, as a novice. Esquinas, however was a knowledgeable sports fanatic, with unusual marketing and communication skills. Eventually, he persuaded Cooper that it would be feasible to build a new state of the art arena on the land Cooper owned in the Sorrento Valley area northwest of San Diego. He also convinced Cooper that a minority led ownership team would have a competitive appeal with the NBA for an expansion franchise. With Cooper's approval, Richard called me at Honeywell and simply said, "let's bring NBA basketball back to San Diego. Richard wanted me and my investors involved in the total project. We eventually reached an agreement that I would be in the basketball franchise business only. For several months we researched the fan base to better understand the resistance we'd receive bringing a new NBA team to that city with a Black owner. All indications were positive regarding me and the race issue. Early on we had the support of my friend Bill Walton, who is loved in that town. We also received a major endorsement from Jack Kemp who was a George Bush senior cabinet member at the time. On one weekend Meadowlark Lemon came in for a fan rally and spoke of our long friendship and travels as teammates. All was going well except the media kept reminding everyone of the past owner experiences. One newspaper version stated " San Diego's most recent NBA entry, the Clippers, purchased in 1981 promised to spare no expense in creating a winner and was soon downsizing and cutting cost." In those days, attendance was never robust and by 1984 the team moved the entire operation to Los Angeles.

In most tragedy you often find humor. The owner of the departed franchise, over dinner one evening, asked me " what makes you think you are qualified to run an NBA franchise?" My wife and Ed Garvey were looking on and nearly choked on their salads. We were sitting on several thousand season ticket deposits in the bank and my investment group had the financing. I answered, "I'm hungry and poor so failure is not an option and I am prepared do what ever it takes."

The NBA commissioner's office never made a commitment but remained objective and supportive. My friend Colangelo provided valuable insights and advice on remaining calm and focused on the long term. However, the overriding concern was with the lead member of the San Diego investment group. He seemed to completely ignore protocol. His transgressions seemed minor on the surface, but often inflammatory to cynical media who already had their patience tested by prior ownership. Esquinas was smart, enthusiastic and on task. When things got off strategy we depended on Richard and his astute wife Kerry to get Cooper and others back on point. Too often these efforts failed.

In a short time I learned a lot and many great friendships were formed. Dennis Mathieson stepped up with several credible introductions; Russ Granik was respectful and forthright through out the process as was David Stern and local sports writer Tom Cushman who always gave solid personal and professional advice.

Lessons learned were many; first was to be prepared for all outcomes followed by taking the time to build a winning team with defined roles. Could we have won – yes; was the opportunity real- to this day I am not certain, would it have been worth the financial risk and effort-absolutely. In the 2012 market that franchise could be worth 3-500 million dollars.

After the San Diego experience; I methodically loosened my association with Honeywell, initiating a leave of absence on December 12, 1994. But this was hardly the end of my involvement in big business deals and transactions. For over a year I'd operated a very profitable "sideline" with the industry's highest ratio of return on capital deployed. It was an enterprise near and dear to my heart: the Harlem Globetrotters.

7 HARLEM GLOBETROTTERS, TAKE TWO

I played my final game as a Harlem Globetrotter in 1964. My experiences as part of that organization were forever etched on my mind, heart and spirit. Only in my wildest dreams could I have imagined that, many years in the future, this organization and I would reunite. But that is exactly what happened – and it really was one wild ride.

While I was pursuing my business career, the Globetrotters had gone through a number of incarnations. On March 15, 1966, team founder and owner Abe Saperstein passed away. Abe had suffered a mild heart attack in Australia during one of the team's around-the-world swings. His ill health deeply saddened the players, who hated to see the world's greatest sports pioneer slow down. Although Abe regained his strength temporarily, he was prepping for prostate surgery when he had a second, fatal heart attack.

In liquidating the assets of Abe's trust, Continental Bank placed a $3.5 million value on the team, a substantial sum for a sports franchise at that time. On June 8, 1967 the team sold for $3.71 million to three young entrepreneurs: Potter Palmer, John O'Neil and soon-to-be managing director George Gillette. After a few turbulent years, the team was then sold to Metromedia, which tried to grow the Globetrotters' audience as a youth-oriented comedic property by way of a very popular and widely remembered television cartoon. The cartoon was based on a formula: Typically, the team would travel somewhere and get involved in a conflict with local villains. The conflict ended up being settled by a basketball challenge. Guess who would win? One can only imagine how shocked and disappointed many in the Black community were – and those my dad's age had already been saddened by the team's increased clowning in the 1950s and '60s.

In introducing the cartoons, Metromedia came up with a profitable way to capitalize on the Globetrotters' legacy and celebrity. But it did not prove sustainable. In the opinion of many, the cartoon era and the ensuing image undermined the essence of this great global brand. Fans forgot the magic of the brand, the power of the basketball team playing on actual regulation courts, and the incomparable style, competitive prowess and unique humor for which the team had become famous.

I was doing my thing at Honeywell. On occasion the topic of great teams would come up, and I would proudly mention the legacy of the Globetrotters. People would reference the animated series. I kept remembering Abe's mantra: "The Globetrotters are first in family entertainment, the best basketball team with some of the best players in the world, and proud ambassadors for all that's good about humankind." You can't imagine the dismay I felt realizing that the most well-known ambassadors of basketball could exit the sports scene as cartoon characters.

By the late 1970s, the world of professional sports had changed dramatically, with televised games impacting the visibility of every league and the manufacturing of stardom of individual players. Superstars were being created electronically in living rooms with slow motion video, camera angles and highlight films on a daily and weekly basis. Everyone and every team seemed to benefit financially from this media, except the Globetrotters. The Globetrotters players complained, and even refused to work at one point. The nation was shocked when America's good-natured clowns turned smiles into frowns over pay and working conditions.

For a decade, the organization went into a decline. Although the NBA was booming, the Globetrotters were considered irrelevant as competitors and stale as entertainers. By the 1980s, the talent level had slipped to a point where the players were a parody of themselves and just about every gimmick imaginable was being tossed at an indifferent public. As it had since Abe Saperstein's death, the brand drifted further away from its idealism and core competency.

Despite all this, according to Ben Green's *Spinning the Globe*, in December 1986 Metromedia sold the franchise for $30 million (an impressive sum for a non-league sports team) to the International Broadcast Company (IBC) in December 1986. IBC was a Minneapolis-based entertainment group that also had under its broad umbrella amusement parks, live theaters and the Ice Capades.

IBC borrowed heavily during the 1980s and the Globetrotters became its cash cow. IBC was so indifferent to the Globetrotters' proud history that, in a panic move for survival, they persuaded Meadowlark Lemon – arguably the most famous Globetrotter of all time, but retired 15 years earlier – to stage a comeback in 1993. This was done not for those fans that remembered cartoon character Meadowlark, and not for the benefit of youngsters who had never seen him play some really magical basketball, but to appease a bankruptcy creditor. During

Meadowlark's time on tour, which lasted 55 games, he frequently contacted me to lament the organization's state of decay.

I could never really blame IBC for the mess left behind by the cartoons. It was all just painful. The team never missed a touring season, but by the time IBC went into Chapter 11 in 1991, the financial drain, coupled with the incredible rival draw of the NBA as a television property, had caused a significant decline in the acceptance of the Harlem Globetrotter product and image.

* * *

In 1992, I began investigating the possibility of buying the team. I had acquired business turnaround skills in corporate America. Although my due diligence confirmed that the Globetrotters' infrastructure had fallen apart, I knew enough about sports economics to be confident that, if retooled and properly marketed, the team could find a viable niche in the growing sports and entertainment world. I had also been thinking about paybacks for the successes life had provided me, and it seemed that a wonderful contribution would be to take an African-American institution of such historical significance, revitalize it, and make certain it would have a future of financial health and positive influence. My family was incredulous. They would ask me, "Why are you wasting your time, money and management skills?" But they came to see it was my dream and my journey.

The bankers rejected my first offer, which was to buy all of IBC, but they did bring me in as a professional advisor to the organization. They wanted me to tell them what to do with the organization to get the most value for it when they finally were ready to sell. At that point, I honestly thought that maybe the team itself should be retired. My hope was to get the team and several former legends enshrined in the Hall of Fame, do a documentary or movie (see *The Team That Changed the World*), have a historically accurate book written about the team (see Ben Green's *Spinning the Globe*), sell licensed merchandise at retail (this was ultimately achieved successfully in a multi-million dollar partnership with FUBU), and even start a global youth foundation. But as for the touring team itself: That was to be history in my earlier visions.

The thing is, when I met with the players, in March of 1993, to tell them just that, I couldn't. When I looked into the eyes of some of the great ones like Tex Harrison, Sweet Lou Dunbar, Meadowlark Lemon and Clyde Sinclair, I suddenly heard myself talking about entertaining families with healthy and skill-based humor, building a respected competitive team, becoming known for doing good, and rebuilding the organization. The players were with me, all the way. The guy who showed up to give a "going out of the basketball business" speech left with a mission: After a nice dinner with Meadowlark and my two daughters at one of Boston's historic seafood and clam chowder restaurants, I raced back to the hotel room to write down everything that had come out of my mouth.

To make sure I was being realistic, I convened 12 trusted associates – former Globetrotters, Red Klotz, an arena owner, and marketing experts from Honeywell. (I was a senior vice president world-wide marketing at Honeywell by then, but I was already involved as a silent owner-investor in other ventures, and I had the full support of Honeywell's CEO.) We met for a three-and-a-half day summit. When it was over, I called the bankers, offering them $5.5 million for the Globetrotters alone (this included a $500,000 personal investment on my part). I was told that compared to other bidders I had articulated the best vision about the organization's potential, and that they would finance $4.5 million. I countered with a proposal giving them a non-voting 20 percent stake for a $1 million line of credit and buy-out clause. They called in 48 hours and agreed after a few clarifications. And just like that, history was made: The first African-American to own a major sports and entertainment company was born in a boxcar in Illmo, Illinois.

The only small matter left was to bring the vision to life.

* * *

In truth, I was so driven by my desire to restore the proud legacy of a sports legend that I greatly underestimated the forces against success. I found that financial restoration came relatively easily, but the competitive pride of the organization had waned, and appreciation for the global goodwill role I envisioned was often met with cynicism. Greed was becoming the new standard in the world of sports, and giving wasn't on the minds of many individuals who had become starstruck and shallow. Good deeds had given way to flash and bling as the new street and media currency.

But I wasn't discouraged; I was the consummate insider who had learned from the team's creator. I was the former player who understood better than most the pinnacle of excellence this team had reached, and what it could mean to kids who were poor and in need of a dream like I had been. I knew the impact this one team could have on the future of the game, as well as current and future players – not to mentions its 350 living alumni.

But I had to face facts: At this point in time the Globetrotters weren't stylish or cool. And, unlike the now-defunct New York Rens, the team had zero urban street swagger. The last of that asset disintegrated with the cartoons.

We wanted to find out, scientifically, exactly where we stood, so we held a series of focus groups. Young people told us they didn't know a thing about us, and many of the older participants hadn't heard of us in years. They asked if we were just clowns, or if we could really play basketball.

I decided we would do whatever it took to become relevant again; we had to find a formula that made us matter. So we showed the audience entertainment, and they loved the non-racial humor, the music and the display of skill. They loved Globie, our mascot, too. But they wanted more evidence that the Globetrotters were good people with unique talents. We quickly ramped up the team's charitable giving, taking a page from the Honeywell playbook and partnering with a dozen foundations. After a couple of years of recruiting and hard work, our coaches had the team prepared to play and defeat many of the world's best amateur and professional teams. We played the NCAA's Syracuse, St John's, University of Connecticut, Purdue, Iowa, Maryland, Ohio State, Minnesota, Michigan State and many others. Can you imagine an annual 14- to 20-game road trip over twenty nights playing this caliber of opponents before sell-out crowds and winning 86 percent of these games over four years against legendary coaches like Gene Keady, Jim Boeheim, Tom Izzo and others? We played and defeated development league teams, college all-star teams at the Final Four, and Dennis Rodman's Streetball All-Stars at the NBA All-Star event. As the team toured Europe, we beat Kareem's All-Stars, a great group of aging legends and Hall of Famers, in 14 of 15 games played. During the NBA lockout in the mid-90s, we put our eight best players together with three professional pick-ups, added Ivory Manning as our coach and won the Los Angeles Pro summer league championship. More importantly, we played good international teams. Abe Saperstein would have been very proud.

The sell-out crowds were conflicted at first, but entertained and pleasantly surprised. This change was hard for many to swallow, for it required a leap of faith and reversal of paradigms, but most fans welcomed the team back as a basketball power relevant to sponsors and promoters. The attendance ratios soared, as did the team's Q-ratings (a measure of popularity and audience familiarity). The ultimate peak reached was in the winter of 2005, when we offered the 2004 Olympic champion Argentine national team $1 million guarantee to play the Harlem Globetrotters for the mythical World Championship, using their Olympic roster and playing under international rules. The three game series was set for a first game in Miami and a second game in Las Vegas all on national television. Chris Clouser had gone to bat to assure the first sell-out in Miami. A third game rubber match was on hold. San Antonio's superstar Ginobli had heroically put his reputation on the line as he saw the match as a major fundraiser for his countries sport. I wanted the cash proceeds and the stage for the Globetrotters and other non league talent around the world. The deal stalled when the Argentines made a push for early cash. We had already agreed to 250k thirty days from tip off and the balance after each game. I said "no" and gave them a deadline to get back in line with our letter agreement. They called three hours after the deadline. I was mistaken; this turned out to be a great opportunity lost because of my firmness and refusal to seek a compromise. We were able to do all these things while playing over 300 games a year with two teams holding a 60 to 70 percent occupancy rate.

* * *

The team's three-week training camps sponsored and paid for by the Disney Corporation became events in themselves. We aspired to have a collection of performers who knew their roles and, through innate skill and repetition, were masters of every aspect of the often complex Globetrotter game of basketball. However, as hard as I tried, I had little to no success getting rid of all the show plays and skits. Thankfully, Tex Harrison, with whom I found it easy to communicate on this subject, convinced everyone to use the few skits remaining to focus on the comedic skills of a few designated players, thus avoiding slapstick and transparent racial gimmicks.

Many of our arena partners said the recruits from 2000 on were stronger, faster and bigger than any player group recruited in over 20 years. Almost all the recruits had some prior professional experience; thanks to our chief recruiter Chad Groth, the vast majority had the pedigree of McDonalds All-Americans and Division I backgrounds. They were a challenge to work with, but my instruction to Chad was that I wanted to see the best available talent in the world – and let me and others worry about the social work.

At one point we had two Division I coaches on the bench, as well as future Memphis Grizzlies NBA Coach of the Year Lionel Hollins, legend Bernie Bickerstaff of the Charlotte Hornets and Washington Wizards, and Phoenix Suns head coach Alvin Gentry. The team's exhibition opposition was led by fiery competitor Red Klotz. I knew Red when I was a kid, and his endorsement and approval of our growth strategies and improvements was all I needed to know that we were on the right track.

We were committed to being the best. To the fans, every night, everything the team did was designed to look smooth, simple and fun. There were many nights when the flow of basketball and the comedic and basketball skill bordered on pure magic. I was asked how the players tolerated 300 games a year and the answer was simple: the love of the game – and the 50 or so nights a year when the gods of performance would shine on the team and everybody and everything would be perfect, making everything worthwhile. Sometimes it happened in Madison Square Garden; sometimes it happened in Duluth, Minnesota or River City. It didn't matter, when you played in such a game of perfection or you paid to see it, you never ever forgot it. The last one I saw was in Lyon, France in 2002.

New players, with few exceptions, had to accept that very few recruits become complete and accomplished Globetrotters overnight. To learn the ball-handling techniques unique to the team's patented style and be able to perform them in the flow of a game takes at least two years to master. Owners and new coaches too often forget this and either over-promote a player or give up too soon on a jewel. I made the mistake with Keiron "Sweet Pea" Shine, only to have Tex bring him back to become one the best all-around stars in team history. Sending Paul "Showtime" Gaffney home as a rookie was my way of giving him a wake-up call as to his potential. I had been in their shoes. I talked about the intensity of stars like Goose and Marques, as well as how demanding Meadowlark could be and how impatient he was with new players (even Wilt Chamberlain). I told them how much time Hallie Bryant and Tex Harrison spent with me when I was a rookie, and how obsessed I became with being a part of the team's "magic circle." In camp, we talked about the sacrifices needed to cultivate sports genius and about mastering basketball moves that caused even teammates, let alone fans, to ask, "How are they doing that?" We readied ourselves to start playing again against the best teams from all over the world. And we perfected "you had to be there" moves that could only be seen at one of our events, like Showbiz Jackson's over-the-back half court hook shots or Michael Wilson's dunking through a 12-foot basket.

Our training also included classes on what would be expected from the new era Globetrotter. We held workshops on the team's legacy and history (in 2000 I hired my old friend Gov Vaughn to be team historian and organize an alumni association). We also had classes on how players were to deal with the public, on how to conduct themselves as role models, and even on money management. We also emphasized how our team members were professional basketball players as well as marketing representatives of a proud and iconic African-American institution. They were required to be positive influences in communities across the country and around the world.

I knew the global market was expanding around sports and the game of basketball, and fans needed an approachable team of role models to embrace in person, not just those seen in footwear ads. Our mission was contemporary relevance, but our formula would be the same one that was laid down by Abe Saperstein – the hands-down master of sports and entertainment fusion – 40 years earlier. We would fuse great basketball (no joke), good fun, innovation and universal goodwill. We were in the business of creating memories, smiles and dreams. So we'd strive to make everything about our product authentic and skill-based – nothing fake, nothing sleazy or insulting, and nothing that we couldn't take to families around the world.

* * *

Although I knew that the Globetrotters would once again be a great "product," I also knew that having a great product is not always enough to sustain a brand. The essence of our success would lie in promotion and in relationships. Good relationships had to be forged with sponsors and, of course, with customers. But I knew I had to start with the media.

We didn't publicize ourselves to the sports pages; we went directly in to pitch the financial writers. I leveraged my business identity with *The Wall Street Journal*, *The New York Times*, *USA Today* and any business editors who were interested in what an African-American Honeywell executive had to say about branding and turnaround strategies.

These were strange times for me personally. I was very publicly visible. For example, in a very short period, maybe 90 days, I made four appearances at the podium of the New York Stock Exchange: once with Honeywell, then with the Executive Leadership Council, later with Stanley Tool as a board member, and finally as the Chief Executive of the Harlem Globetrotters. That in itself might be a new record for ringing the bell and eating canapés in the big NYSE boardroom.

The publicity that resulted had an upside slant on future business possibilities that was vital in attracting future corporate partners. The Globetrotters were, quite simply, a good story. People are naturally curious about them: Who are these guys? Are they really that good? How can they be having so much fun after all these years? If there is one thing I learned, it's that people will sample a wide range of branded offerings if the story is appealing and the storyteller is credible.

Re-establishing our brand was so essential that I became relentless about it. Former players still tell a story about a time in 1994 when the team was about to kick off its first U.S. tour. The team, which was headquartered in California, and my executive staff, which was based in Minneapolis, were to gather in the first of 100 scheduled cities to make certain that all the travel elements were well-organized. I was waiting for the team bus to pull up so we could go to the arena for a pregame practice when my assistant Colleen Linehan noticed the Globetrotters showed up in a purple bus with the words "VIP Lounge" written along the side. Everyone still remembers the horrified look on my face. I asked, "Why isn't the bus wrapped with the Harlem Globetrotters' tour logo and sponsor logos?" Jeff Munn, our Vice President of Operations, replied, "Well Chief, we were told by our CFO to cut costs, and that would cost $12,000."

I sat each and every person involved in the tour down and explained the importance of branding, and how the tour buses would act as a traveling billboard carrying our brand through hundreds of towns and cities across America. I then reminded our CFO that I used the team and marketing staff to make the numbers she recorded. Within three days the bus was newly wrapped. That $12,000 was a drop in the bucket compared to the return the company got for the reach and the constant signage displayed on those buses for three solid months.

It's critical to know how to allocate your resources. That's why one of the other things I did early on was cut our advertising budget in half and use that money to hire regional marketing people. Year round, these marketers met with arena managers, arena marketing staffs and local businesses that wanted to promote our events. The arena people did a better job of promoting us, alerted us to group sales opportunities, and helped connect us with sponsors and local media.

In addition, our regional marketing people would identify the leading charity in the cities we'd visit, reach out, and say, "We're coming to your town. What can we do for you?" For instance, sometimes I would donate my time and speak at an organization's annual fundraiser.

Our social commitment – a central tenet of our brand – took many, many forms. Our players would visit hospitals, schools and youth clubs year round. We put on 25 or 30 camps each summer, sponsored by

Disney, Burger King and Western Union, and made a special point of helping disadvantaged kids, many of whom didn't have to pay anything at all.

Our public affairs department agenda included annual appearances at military locations in Asia and Iraq, and meetings with heads of state and religious leaders such as Nelson Mandela, Prince Charles and Pope John Paul. (We made the Pope an honorary Globetrotter – surely a historical first – and, after a whirlwind tour of London businesses, I presented Prince Charles with team jerseys for both his sons.) We donated large sums of money to causes, relief efforts and activist organizations, supporting, among others, the American Red Cross, the NAACP, PUSH, UNICEF, Habitat For Humanity and the ANC (South Africa's African National Party).

At one point, David Bell, one of nation's leading advertising CEOs and brand experts, came to me with an idea to use the Globetrotters to build a $1 billion charitable war chest. I liked his idea. I felt it was achievable with help from a few foreign governments and several million in seed dollars from large corporations. The Globetrotters would kick the 20-year charitable initiative off with a $100 million commitment in memory of Abe Saperstein.

* * *

Since I was still with Honeywell during my early years of running the Globetrotters, I was working 24/7. On Friday nights, I'd fly out to various Globetrotter offices and meet with people all day Saturday and Sunday. In one of those meetings, I said we were going to play in the U.K. and then spread the team out across Europe. I asked for a pan-European strategy that projected the investment in Year 1 for profits in Years 2, 3 and 4. I spoke about this for over an hour, then went home to Minneapolis. Monday morning my phone rang. My vice president of marketing for the Globetrotters said, "I hope you don't mind if I ask you a question, but what's a strategy?" I returned the next week and started teaching classes on the basics. I wanted every player to retire after no more than 15 years healthy, financially secure and prepared to get on with their lives after basketball while there was still time and youth to build families and a second career. As a business turnaround, this was to become my most challenging goal especially in the get-rich-quick time we lived in. I failed at this, even though salaries escalated 200-300% and we matched 401K saving plans by 50% and eventually 100%. My controller would pitch this program and other wealth-development efforts every year and fewer than a third of the players would sign up. If I had it to do over again, I'd find better ways to achieve this goal.

In my own case, my patience gave out one day when, after working hundreds of hours a month for two years booking and promoting dates, and selling sponsorships while traveling thousands of miles without a pay day, I thought it time I receive a salary. I went to my board and made my case; they listened and eventually assigned an investment banker to come up with a fair number. Six months later I was presented with the a salary amount. If I'd taken it, I would have been the 10th-hghest employee on the payroll list, right next to my team's new assistant coach. My ego exploded! (To put it in perspective, that next weekend I presented the South Carolina NAACP with a $50,000 personal check; it was more than I would have netted from the proposed annual salary.) I just quietly refused the pay increase, took participation in a revenue-based management fee and began plans to do a generous buyout of all the investors and board members.

Soon after that, and once I left Honeywell, we were able to purchase more of the company in a series of cash-out deals. In 1995, one of our major lending banks closed its U.S. operations and sold off its loans. We were able to buy their 20 percent ownership shares for a fraction of the original asking price and market value, because of the timing. After more buyouts in 2002, I took on 100% of the next risk level alone, carrying just the players' 401Ks, the executive staff's preferred stock and a traditional retail pay-as-you-go bank partner as outstanding liabilities. There was no one left to second-guess or look over our shoulders. I wanted to take care of the players and staff and grow the organization by reinvesting profits into charities and improving the company. These kinds of goals don't sit well with investors and particularly private equity firms. That was a scary moment, but I was making money while flying without a net. I had found that the more investors we had, the more the distractions and oversight. This was inefficient and disruptive; every investor seemed capable of finding a money manager or lawyer willing to waste our valuable time. This was true regardless of the amount invested. One investor put up just $5,000 and I personally gave him $12,500 in return. His ex-wife's divorce attorney called for weeks to review the company books.

Now, in theory at least, the future of the organization was in my hands. By 2005 the team had achieved a list of unparalleled accomplishments. Its sports Q-ratings were ahead of Michael Jordan's and were topped only by those of Tiger Woods. The company also had a 10-year average annual growth rate of 14 percent. But the historic revival of the Globetrotters would not have happened without help from so many. Dennis Mathisen was my mentor and friend and also the deal expert who was willing to be the organization's financial backstop. At a recent luncheon I asked him what his reason was for taking so much risk. His response was, "I believed in you and wanted to be a part of a meaningful social mission." Chris Clouser gave us our first sponsorships sight unseen, and later introduced us to over $30 million worth of corporate sponsor dollars that included Burger King, Western

Union and the Campbell Soup Company. Paul Fireman, Chairman of Reebok and one of the best corporate chairpersons in America, gave the Globetrotters a generous five-year shoe and apparel deal, validating us as an authentic global sports entity. Paul cared about diversity in Reebok's customer base, its management team and its board of directors, which, through Peter Robey, he invited me to join. Ed Garvey, co-founder of the NFL players association, was our team attorney and a close personal friend; he was also my "light house" of integrity for all business dealings. In Ed's reign with the Harlem Globetrotters, we never had disruptions in labor, or nuisance lawsuits, or chronic contractual misunderstandings. Our personal banker, Linda Netjes, kept her heart open and her management at arm's length.

Finally, there's Oprah Winfrey. There are so many wonderful and different versions of the story as to how she grew excited about booking the Globetrotters on her syndicated daytime show that I won't choose one to report. However it came to be, the team was invited to make an appearance that turned into two days of Oprah featuring the Harlem Globetrotters, and closed with an unequivocal endorsement of the team's family values, its global barnstorming legacy, and its charitable accomplishments. Afterward it was like a light switch flipped. After those appearances, Globetrotter attendance rose sharply, as did our corporate giving and my own personal commitment to causes around the world. Life around the home office was never to be the same, and we all became grateful members of Oprah's fan club.

Of all the wonderful things that happened to the Globetrotters while I was at the helm, the most gratifying of all began in 2001 when Basketball Hall of Fame Chairman and iconic player and coach David Gavitt pulled me aside during the Hall of Fame enshrinement. Dave said, "We have something in common. We both know today's Hall of Fame is not a complete picture of basketball's greatest teams and players without the Harlem Globetrotters. I promise you we'll fix this."

The team was inducted in 2002. I stood center stage with Coach Gavitt and accepted the honor. After a big and sincere hug on national TV, all I could do was to thank Dave on behalf of the Saperstein family and 400-plus alumni. David was a friend and an honorable man. He had the guts to do what no other before him had ever done: acknowledge the central role the Globetrotters had played in the sport of basketball since their founding in 1926.

Before closing this bit of my story, I want readers to understand the lesson I learned regarding the importance of selection of business partners. Once you make a partner selection, you should work as hard and as honestly as possible to make the partnership succeed. However, when you discover there is either no partnership or you have NO VOICE, then it's time to conduct a thorough self-assessment before you decide to move on, or as LeBron James said "take your talents to the beach" (somewhere it will be appreciated). That simple fact has become life lesson 101.

After 14 years of Globetrotter ownership, I reached a point where I felt it was time to step aside. After consideration, I believed there were others with more capital and resources than myself to create the innovations needed for long-term sustainable growth. After reviewing the economic climate, we put the team up for auction using Green, Holcomb and Fischer, a highly regarded Minneapolis company. There were dozens of respondents and the finalists put very strong purchase price proposals together. With the price issue settled, we did a flip-flop and conducted strategic interviews with each of the finalists; 30 days later, my advisors recommended selling 80% interest in the team to Shamrock Holdings – a company founded by the Roy E. Disney family investment firm.

Within weeks after the sale, the company encountered internal cynicism, distrust and control issues (and the company's focus was consumed with the accounting and reporting systems as they were being revamped). This system had been installed 10 years earlier by Marshall Finance, former Honeywell Controller Ruth Busta, and had been refined over the years by company Controller and finance guru Mike Syracause into an industry standard. The scary part was the new private equity leaders never listened; not to me, the former owner, or arguably to the best financial and operating team in the industry. They quickly used their position power and assumed the role as teachers of a business they had never seen up close. This was bothersome because I was an owner who was also a former player. During my tenure, the company and staff had sold over $80 million in multi-year sponsorships with gross sales of over $70 million in licensing. The team also had 14 consecutive years of growth averaging 14%. After two years under the new private equity leadership, the aforementioned statistics almost disappeared and the attendance capacity ratios started dropping.

I was prepared, and qualified, to comment on the state of this business. At Honeywell, I had been a venture executive (acquiring companies and repositioning old and new businesses). On that job I earned business unit executive of the quarter six times and runner-up for general manager of the year three times. In addition, I served on the board of directors of 10 private and public companies. Finally, as the Trotters' largest single shareholder and its non-executive chairman, I was capable and motivated to help restart the growth of the Globetrotters. When I stated this in a board meeting, I saw heads dropping as someone broke the silence and asked "What would you do on your first day?" Before I could answer with A) create a three-year strategic marketing plan (which eventually happened two years later); B) staff for accountability; and C) reconstitute this board, there was a condescending compliment followed by an urgent call for adjournment to catch flights to the East and West Coast.

The Globetrotters are a great company, an even greater brand, with a competent CEO and proven staff. But five years had passed. Growth, innovations and overall performance continued to be stalled, capacity ratio declined and valuation was not increasing. I'm told, some of the senior staff members were threatened with discipline if they talked to me. At one board meeting, the directors were instructed not to talk to employees. One of my friends sold a highly valued NBA franchise and the newspapers frequently report similar behaviors and circumstances.

All this was hard to deal with, especially in light of the money I had been paid for the company a few years earlier, and the psychological bias I have for winning. Finally, as the largest single shareholder and non-executive chairman, I wanted to help. I had believed in the vision of Roy Disney and the immense credibility and track record of the affable and brilliant Stanley Gold. After a couple years, I found it hard for my corporate style of personal accountability to function in this particular private equity environment. In my opinion, the new leadership lost ground not because they ignored me, but because they had no related experience; and they could not appreciate the scale of the business complexities and subtleties. In other words, they simply didn't know what they didn't know. These kind of unchecked collisions of egos and behaviors happen, as I also fell victim to it at Honeywell but was quickly set straight by my boss at the time, Bill Wray.

The media once called to fact check a Globetrotter manager's statement "that since I had millions put away I no longer cared and had lost interest." Everyone who knows me would disagree because none of that rings true. It's possible I had nothing of interest to offer these people and their success plans. But to not care – no way! There is a part of me that will always be with the Globetrotters and a part of the Trotters that will forever be with me. I want the organization to succeed because the team represents an important part of the Jackson family legacy. I also believe in what the organization should stand for and I still believe a contemporary interpretation of Abe Saperstein's intentions would be the surest way for the organization to achieve its potential. To this day, I take every opportunity to memorialize Abe and the team's legends and superstars. My family production company's Boxcar Entertainment partnered with Team Works Media of Chicago to produce a documentary called "GOOSE" highlighting the legacy and contributions of 2011 Hall of Famer Reece "Goose" Tatum. The young stars of Abe's era not only built the legacy of this great franchise, but also played a significant role in, quite literally, leveling the playing field for Blacks in all of professional sports. My Globetrotter management formula was a classic brand-building effort; find your history (intentions), your strengths, and match them with a market where you matter.

The satisfying outcome for me came in August 2011. I had a private dinner with a Shamrock executive and it turned into a productive exchange of ideas and critiques. I read to him a list of 12 priorities and I also outlined things I believed were underachieving, and several items and approaches that should be changed and/or implemented. After listening and reading over the suggestions, he extended his hand, we shook and he said thank you. We wished each other well and he actually asked for a copy of my comments and notes. We shook hands again and headed to the ball park to watch an Arizona Diamondbacks baseball game together. Life, as well as working relationships, will often run in cycles. And survivors learn this.

My take-away from this experience and the nearly 20-year journey in the sports business and most of that time with the Globetrotters, is as follows: Just for a moment, visualize the unintended consequences of segregation – where great lawyers, scientists, musicians, artists, writers, photographers, educators, entrepreneurs, future Presidents and sports stars were relegated to second-class citizenship because of the color of their skin or the texture of their hair and shamelessly kicked out of the mainstream simply because those who controlled the purse strings happened to be the storytellers in their time. And think of the story that would have unfolded if the NBA had retained its segregated ways – the 20 best Black players in the world in 2012 would be divided between the fabulous New York Rens and the Harlem Globetrotters. The Reverend Jesse Jackson said it best, "Had the NBA and NCAA remained segregated, we may never have known how great the multi-billion dollar game of basketball could become."

No one knows these truths better than the current enlightened NBA commissioner, David Stern.

8 MY LATEST, GREATEST DREAMS

My life has been, and continues to be, an incredible, improbable journey. Throughout its twists and turns, my father would sometimes ask me, "Who taught you, and where did you get the big ideas you seem to constantly have?" He would also say, "Buddy boy, I want you to write a book one day. You've done and seen a lot, and you know how much I love to read. I'll be your first customer."

Sadly, Emmett Jackson died on June 23, 2011 at the age of 91, before this book's final draft was complete – but not before I was able to answer his question about where my dreams came from. They came from him, and from those before him. I dreamed of growing up to be like my grandfather and my dad; a dream of being responsible, being looked up to and respected as a role model and a leader. Later, as I glimpsed the world of business, the possibility of economic independence became a part of my focus. My goals of being socially active and affecting public policy began to crystallize when I met the young Reverend Jesse Jackson while in college.

But still, I so often think back to my parents. What must it have been like for them and other young African-Americans in the 1940s and 50s? What could the source of their dreams and hopes have been?

Those were extremely dismal days, with the scarring of post-slavery fully exposed to a nation that had just fought a world war on foreign soil to protect other nations' freedoms. What did they see that inspired them? There was no Internet, no TV, very little travel, and certainly few role models as we know them today. To what, other than survival, did they aspire? Could a family or individual earning $10 or $20 a week aspire to see the world one day? Did they understand the value of education? And what did an impoverished family tell its children about the old days when slavery and racial cruelties were their grandparents' dominant reality?

I tried many times to have this conversation with my father in recent years. I'd ask, "Would you dare to dream of one day living in or owning those big houses you worked in? Was getting an advanced education a meaningful or operative concept?" He'd answer, "Well, in the good old days, things were easier to understand because what we experienced and what we were allowed to hope for was limited to basic stuff like taking care of family, hard work, good food, music, health, avoiding being lynched, and basically just staying alive."

I believe when my father and those of his generation were young, they exploited the benefits of youth, which puts a mask on a lot of tough stuff. By the time they had kids and understood the consequences of the damage that America's apartheid had done, they were either old and tired, or ignored. Also, for my dad and his cohorts, things were relatively more peaceful and painless than they had been for their own elders. Back then because of the depression era (or the panic as it was often referred to) if you just had a decent job, there were always worse times behind you.

During our conversations, I asked my dad who the big dreamers of his day were. He said mostly men of faith, and often the schoolteachers. "Nobody would read much in those days, but those of us who did were looked upon as threatening to poor white people and as a little odd, or at least different." Then he added, "There was status in reading back in those days and of course there were wisecracks made. But for the most part, my co-workers and buddies were proud of readers and most weekends I'd spend time teaching or interpreting letters and legal documents for friends. I can't say whether we were different because we read, or we read because we were different."

My grandfather would complain that books in good shape were often hard to come by, and it was rare to see a collection of any size in the home of a Black family. My grandfather Jackson could remember hearing firsthand stories of horrific consequences of a Black person running away to learn reading and writing. My father could speak firsthand about those offering their bodies and lives to usher in decent schooling and desegregated or separate but equal teaching and learning environments. And both always spoke proudly about seeing me attending and graduating from a university. Neither was as concerned about where I'd go in sports as they were about the education. Sadly, I was never made aware of this. Somehow, though, a few Black families like mine would set enough money aside to purchase a set of encyclopedias as a reminder that education and knowledge were paths to better times. Still, Granddad always found his books and newspapers, my dad recalled, and would read and doze all day every Sunday. My uncles would joke that reading like that took away valuable sleep time and would contend that Old Man Jackson always fell asleep while reading, so why not just start out sleeping? But, naps aside, throughout the next week, you would hear my

Granddad quoting something he had read or asking questions to further what he'd learned.

Granddad was pretty smart and those around him knew it – but more importantly he was a well-read man. He liked history and characters from the past, but he hated novels, calling them "books of liars." He was also intrigued by how things worked, and that curiosity made him a really good fixer and builder. As the neighborhood "bootleg engineer," he accumulated hundreds of sophisticated tools for all kinds of labor as he and my dad became proficient welders. My grandfather built the home he lived in until his death June 21, 1961, and half a dozen others in and around the neighborhood. He was proud of the homes and treated them like his children. Once he built or repaired a home, he was constantly inspecting and upgrading as he seemed always on emergency call. When my grandfather retired after nearly 35 years at the American Steel Foundry working as an engineer's assistant, he was allowed to enroll in a local engineering school to become a master draftsman who would be knowlegeble in the preparation and reading of architectural blueprints.

Dad noted that Granddad wasn't thrilled when I started playing basketball. His complaint was that I no longer seemed to have an interest in reading or sitting with him on Sundays. I remember hearing him fuss about that at times. Of course, it would have been hard for my grandfather to envision what lay ahead for me, but I credit him with instilling in both my father and me a comfort level in pursuing knowledge. As my dad put it, "In those days we weren't taught how to dream in the way you mean now. But I suppose if you could read and comprehend; one's imagination could carry you just about anyplace."

* * *

How did a person of my background escape a boxcar beginning and land on the privileged side of life's tracks? Even with the many strong good family examples I had, the odds against success of any magnitude were astronomical. Even today seeing a Black president in the White House – something that in my wildest dreams I never thought I'd live to see – and the emergence of so many other Black role models and heroes in politics, entertainment, business, sports and science, I don't lose prospective that progress for minorities has been miniscule when you study the rates of incarceration, poverty, unemployment, school drop-outs, homeless and untimely deaths. So, why me?

Although I can't answer that question with certainty, my good fortune seems to stems from the role models I chose to emulate, my family, the opportunity for education, and finding something early in life that I became passionate about. So looking forward, my family will use our capital to do whatever it takes to lessen the odds for the next generation. One dream for my future has me using whatever clout or wealth I've accumulated over the years to help others over the various obstacles and barriers that stand in the way of their dreams. We live in a free and faith-based society, where America's world leadership has not been based solely on military might. Rather it has been based on hope, and on a shared belief that we are all better off when the least of us has access to education, health care and, most importantly, productive work.

Bridging achievement gaps in education is critical. At the college level, the approach I favor is based on a creative method used at the University of Illinois. Initiated by Dean Tanya Gallagher, former University of Illinois President Joe White, and the program's tireless administrator, Associate Dean Sheri Shaw, this leadership development program incorporates mentoring, communication, social responsibility, goal setting, collaboration skills and guided self-exploration. The Jackson family supports this program, which is now known as the Mannie Jackson Illinois Academic Enrichment and Leadership Program (I-Leap).

I-Leap takes first-generation, underrepresented students and helps them graduate using the kind of mentoring and coaching efforts that I was fortunate to receive throughout my career. Students from various academic disciplines and diverse backgrounds learn to work in groups as they master the arts of critical thinking and problem solving. In less than five years, I-Leap has produced results that are nothing short of miraculous. Graduation rates, grade point averages and civic engagement among its several hundred student participants have exceeded all expectations – not to mention campus norms. In 2009, I-Leap received the Outstanding Advising Program Award, only the second program in Illinois history to receive this national honor. Nearly 10 percent of the program's students received perfect grades in the spring semester of 2010, and 70 percent had higher than a B average. Today the program is producing scholars and future leaders from all social-economic backgrounds.

I see the results from I-Leap and I know that our investment is already achieving positive returns. I want programs like this to be a valued resource for young men and women who hope to enter the worlds of economics, education, health care and public policy. I want them to enter those worlds with confidence and a sense of purpose. I also dream and wish that every student and child will have a Joe Lucco, John Watson, Wes McMurray, Dennis Mathisen, Earl Lloyd, Joe White or Ed Spencer in their lives to care about and inspire them and support their dreams. It's vital to my legacy that I make my BOXCAR TO BOARDROOMS story and mentoring a part of the game plan for the next generation.

Each young person needs to understand the real world we live in. They also need to have a window into the imperfect but usually well-intentioned workplace and its various systems, from an insider's viewpoint, as early as possible. I want to encourage young people from all backgrounds to enter the adult world with a sense of confidence, pride and enthusiasm. Rather than being self-conscious about their own unique stories, I hope they will learn to use their stories and backgrounds as a way to bring perspective to their life planning and to craft unique strategies of combating institutional roadblocks often built into the infrastructure of democracy and capitalism.

Though our system has its flaws, I want future generations to think of capitalism as a positive term; as a reference to opportunities in a free market where everyone who is willing to work hard, build trust and take risk has access to its rewards. I also dream that while they should value what they earn and acquire, they will understand there are even greater rewards in sharing.

* * *

I have certainly come to believe that fulfilling dreams of wealth and independence becomes more possible if one is "out there" in the world, rather than waiting for opportunity to come knocking. When I talk to young people about this principle, I give many examples from my own life. I mention how a speech I gave at Reebok to that company's Black employees resulted in an introduction to the company's owner, Paul Fireman, and soon thereafter an invitation to join the Reebok Board of Directors. I also tell of hand-delivering a $25,000 donation to the Children's Theater and, in doing so, meeting its board chairman, which resulted in an invitation to a dinner party where I was randomly seated next to noted financier, banker and humanitarian Dennis Mathisen, the theater's non-executive president. A 30-year friendship and business relationship began that night.

Meeting top airline executive Chris Clouser through a mutual friend was another amazing connection that resulted in multi-million dollar business ties. Even the Globetrotters appearance on Oprah began with a serendipitous encounter when a member of my staff met one of Oprah's accountants at a local Chicago health club.

The thing is, you never know whom you will meet or how you can help one another. These encounters happen at all stages of life – particularly when you learn to frequent positive places where positive people hang out. It's important to stay open and positive, because while luck may open a door, you still have to be prepared and willing to walk through it.

I also believe strongly that few things are more beneficial than studying the masters in one's chosen field of interest (and, if possible, studying under them or working directly for them). So, in my personal mentoring I also enjoy sharing examples of people from ordinary circumstances who overcame obstacles to move onward and upward. I often talk about the clothing company FUBU (For Us By Us), where four young Black men under age 25 changed the fashion world by attacking an untapped emerging global fashion market head on (and taking my company along for an exciting $70 million ride). The founders believed, rightly, that their understanding and interpretation of the urban fashion market represented the needs of millions of potential customers and clients. The name For Us By Us was built on a concept of self-respect that showed how individuals could better carry their talent and influence while dressed in a manner in which they felt most comfortable. FUBU's genius was in finding a way for urban fashion to display confidence and power. I had the good fortune of getting to know the company's founder and CEO, Daymond John, and I admired his work and his persona so much so that I took a leap of calculated faith and placed a bet on him and his team. I've never regretted the decision and only wished that for all the success we had together I could have gotten to know him better and perhaps done another deal.

Daymond, whose own must-read book is called *Display of Power,* is a good example of the power of entrepreneurship. Starting in the corporate world does not mean you have to finish there. Employees have the option to think of the corporate world as a basic training ground in which to acquire the experience and training necessary to develop their own privately held company.

People want and need jobs to live, learn and develop. Not all first jobs need to be overly exciting, but every job must give us something we need to learn and build upon. If not, leave it fast. Seek careers that offer three things: happiness, personal fulfillment and – most importantly – the prospect of future independence. As a private owner you have all three, as well as the opportunity to eliminate the bureaucracy, random bias and politics of many large companies (particularly those that are publicly held). Ownership is no cakewalk, but it ensures the best chance of being self-directed and of eliminating the burden of constant oversight, as well as the satisfaction of creating value – particularly when your company involves products and services of your own creation. Of course, it also affords the best opportunity to become independently wealthy and benevolent.

If it sounds like I am beating the drums on behalf of entrepreneurialism, I am. But one has to be able to tolerate risk. The truth is, you simply cannot assume that anything good will happen without risk. Next to passion and hard work, risk assumption is the second-most important currency of private ownership.

If you hit walls with one company, one field of work, or even in one geographic area, don't be afraid to keep moving until you find a situation that works for you. As my good friend Novellus CEO Rick Hill said, "Life is simple. Find something to do and a place you care about, and get deeply involved. Use your mind, your work and good intention to make you a better, happier, passionate person and leader."

Another friend, Doug Conant, chairman of the Campbell Soup Company, opines in his book *Touch Points*, "Some leaders say, 'It's not personal; it's just business.' Don't buy it! This means that some leaders believe that to show strength, you need to be tough-minded and tough-hearted. But the opposite is the case. What takes real courage is to make your work intensely personal: to care about your work and about the people you work with. We believe that when you use your heart, you will make better judgments concerning the issue, you will make stronger connections with the other people, and you will develop your personal authority as a leader."

Enlightened companies in the United States have moved toward Doug's perspective. They consider all employees stakeholders, and they stress collaboration over competition. But this philosophy and the behaviors it engenders need to become more widespread in all levels of society, and not just top down. It must begin in your family, schools and communities. Work with your friends, family and co-workers to define winning based on shared responsibility and risk.

It is also important to remember that money and other rewards should and will always follow growth in value. Don't let yourself get distracted from the rules of basic economics: Value placed on goods and services is determined by a free market standard of supply and demand as well as by the options a buyer has. We all know, for example, that fresh tomatoes sold in Minnesota are of greater value when local production is lowest – say, in February. But value is also created when a product's uniqueness and quality are high. The NBA thrives not just because there are only 30 teams in the entire world, but also because their players are exceptional and uniquely skilled at doing something people value. When a great or needed product is both unique and scarce, or when a product exceeds the buyer's expectation, its value rises and its owner is rewarded. As consumer satisfaction increases, so does the desire to have that product. As long as the product is consistent, it will likely own the loyalty of premium-paying consumers.

Maybe my talking about products seems a little impersonal. But remember that people also can become synonymous with "brands." Great all-star baseball players, like baseball player Albert Pujols, are rewarded as brands – because they too are unique, consistent and exceed the expectations of the norm. It's true that not everyone will become a household name, but within one's chosen field, everyone can strive to be singular and reliable and to over-deliver on expectations.

* * *

Reporters ask me all the time if owning the Globetrotters was my biggest dream and accomplishment. I say no. Operating them successfully and having my family become wealthy and socially conscious enough to give back to those in need are my biggest accomplishments. In the past 15 years, my family has made significant financial donations, not only the $2 million to I-Leap but also to other programs at the University of Illinois. We donated $5 million to the Museum for African Art in Harlem to secure an exhibit on Nelson Mandela, as a point of inspiration and education. In my hometown of Edwardsville, Illinois, we've worked with the mayor, superintendent of schools, and the Lincoln School Foundation to support future scholars and youth programs with $2 million. We gave the Naismith Memorial Basketball of Fame a million dollars, its largest grant to date, to promote, recognize and educate people about the good in the sport of basketball and about giving back to their communities. We also support the Rainbow Foundation for needy youth in Chicago; Team Heart, a surgical youth project in Rwanda; and cancer research initiatives all over the country. There have been many gifts given and more to come as the family foundation focuses more clearly on its philanthropic mission to help provide health care, nutrition and education to children and families of color.

Yet for all of this, I am well aware that no single individual, family or foundation can generate all the solutions we need. Today our country faces another dangerous cultural crisis that is not set exclusively along racial lines. Decades of failed leadership and greed have given rise to voices of the so-called "have nots," which sound a lot like those of the civil rights uprisings of the 1950s and '60s. Looking at the demographic facts from the book *Black Americans at the Crossroads*, the unemployment rate among the poor exceeds 50 percent, the number of those flunking out of school exceeds 40 percent, and Blacks own less than one percent of all business outlets. Death rates among babies from impoverished mothers is three times the national average. From the gaps in home foreclosures to family income gaps to the comparative incarceration of the poor, it seems clear a crisis is upon us that requires all hands and all leaders on deck. There is clear evidence of a growing lack of hope, motivation and direction. This requires the energy and the goodwill of Black, White, male, female, the rich and the poor. The election of our current president was, in my opinion, a mandate and urgent cry from the masses to fix our country's problems or else be prepared to face the consequences.

Have everyone you know read my story and the story of others who overcame odds. Promote the need for advocates, mentors and formal education. Reward positive leaders who have a track record of helping the poor and the disadvantaged. We cannot squander this time.

If the United States is to remain viable in an increasingly dangerous world, we'll need to utilize and respect all human resources. Liberal versus conservative ideology presents the same problems as the politics of segregation and prejudice: Both cause us to focus too much on our differences. We are all occupants of a planet that is, in effect, shrinking. The fundamental energy resources we demand need to be shared and utilized rationally if we are to survive as a species. I dream that there will not be a winner-take-all mentality as we face the future. I dream that we will discover mutually beneficial beliefs and that there will be good decisions shared by all who share the limited resources of Earth. I dream and hope that one day we will believe firmly that we are in fact our brothers' keepers.

9 MANNIE'S WORDS OF WISDOM

When it comes to personal and business conduct, an individual's philosophy is shaped over time. In my case, I very consciously used my time to observe. I found there was no value in looking for what my organizational superiors did wrong; it was far more productive to study the many things they did right. The study of leadership behaviors was one of my most enjoyable pastimes in corporate life. I watched how people solved problems, how they made decisions, how they weighed ethical dilemmas. When I give speeches around the country, people are often surprised to hear me say, "Ninety percent of what I learned to succeed in the boardrooms of the world came from my high school basketball coach.

More than a decade after I joined the business world in 1980, I was still learning survival and performance protocols from several smart, successful and caring leaders. (Although, to be frank, I had a few business associates whose company I enjoyed socially but who would never serve as business role models for me.) Among people I deemed most successful and admirable, I discovered an amazing commonality of styles, and these eventually became the cornerstones of my own approach. Over the years, mostly through trial and error, I eventually identified specific philosophies and practices with which I felt most comfortable. Then I practiced being consistent in their application. For example, I never want to rush into any decision, large or small. Whether you are on the basketball court or in the boardroom, take a break, go to the sideline and study the alternatives. Set your personal clock to fit your capability, not the opponents'. In life, sports and business, speed (time) is often the most valued asset of all. But remember to use it the right way; the adage of "speed kills" applies in life, business and sports. Time should be viewed as currency in decision-making; therefore, spend it wisely.

I learned to navigate any confrontation by taking a deep breath and imagining that I am 30,000 feet above the situation. From there I get a better look at problems and possible outcomes from all angles and perspectives. When I occasionally deviated from doing this, I typically experienced the negative consequences of knee-jerk reactions, but I learned over time to simply apologize and reset the clock.

I also learned the value of adaptation. For example, my friend Bill Wray was my boss and mentor. I learned a lot from him, but as my supervisor he annoyed me greatly by starting each day at 6:00 a.m. By doing this he gained a running start on everyone and crafted the day's priorities before I got out of bed. I loved the guy, but I knew that in order to survive I had to find a way to adjust. (To me this was similar to an opposing basketball team playing a zone defense, which requires the offense to adapt.) So, I set my alarm for 5:30 a.m. and quickly organized and studied my work by subject matter. As much as possible, I started each day with my own questions for Mr. Wray – putting me on offense and positioned to learn from his answers, rather than being annoyed by the questions asked by the master.

As I near the end of my boxcar to boardroom journey, I'd like to share with you some additional strategies, beliefs and philosophies that have worked nearly 100 percent of the time for me over the years. A few are pretty basic and require almost no explanations. Like: Don't take or touch any money that you even suspect has come from illegal or unethical practices. And: Don't burn a bridge you may need in the future for a graceful retreat.

Hard-line positions are for the movies. Movie plots end in 90 minutes; life and careers go on for decades in a relatively small world. You'll need all the allies you can hold onto as the years go by. I like telling young people that I've amassed a personal fortune learning from other people. I am wary of those who are constantly teaching or lecturing, because all my adult life I've tried to approach every event as a learning opportunity. The more I learn the better quality questions I can ask of a person or situation. For all of my adult life I have seen myself as a student, asking "What else do I need to know to make the best decisions?" Tex Harrison, the legendary Harlem Globetrotter and coach, could be heard every year shouting out to a rookie having problems, "Son, the more I teach you the dumber I get." I've spent a lot time over years contemplating that intended humorous message and unintended words of wisdom.

Now here are some strategies that require a bit more elaboration:

Showing Up

It was Woody Allen who said that 90 percent of success is created simply by showing up. And it was I who said to my Globetrotter players, "Being late is simply not an option." To me, in a more specific sense, showing up means being wherever your "personal brand" needs to handle your obligations, meet people and engage. This will surely require some sacrifices, since there are times when you would rather be elsewhere. But you simply can't win unless you are playing.

As I review my own brand and career, it is astonishing how many significant relationships I built and maintained in this manner – being places I needed to be in both mind and body, helping someone I hadn't planned on helping, or being a part of some activity that was outside my comfort zone. I especially remember the stepping stones that were placed for me when I showed up for John Watson, Earl Lloyd, Ed Spencer and Dennis Mathisen.

In an earlier chapter, I mentioned my New York Technical Tape Corporation basketball experience. Although my primary responsibility was to be a member of the company's Industrial League basketball team, my next obligation for the pay I received was to become a productive professional employee. By becoming curious about the business and becoming acquainted with one of the company executives, I was offered a companion opportunity in the customer service department. I was given this assignment because I went out of my way to attend every training class and every staff meeting – always arriving early – before I even had the job assignment. In a sense, this was the genesis of my business career.

Cultivate Saturday Morning Relationships

Obviously it's beneficial to become professionally familiar with employees, peers, customers and superiors. How those relationships develop can be critical to success. A "Saturday morning" relationship, however, is a phrase I use to denote the currency of familiarity in my business dealings. Harvey MacKay, a friend and successful entrepreneur, lecturer and author introduced me to the phrase. Good relationships, he explained, can be measured by a hypothetical Saturday morning unannounced call. How would it make you feel to initiate it? What's the reaction on the other end of the line? Test it in your mind. You'll know if the value you place on the relationship is shared and whether the mutual benefit you may one day need from the relationship will be there.

Use This Formula: Real, Win, Worth

My friend Dr. Norm Sidley, one the very best strategic consultants in sales and marketing that I've ever known, would use the phrase "real, win, worth" to describe a process of evaluating relationships and investment opportunities. It can be applied to both business and personal life. The maxim has three basic components:

Before you invest valuable time, energy and capital in any situation, begin by asking: Is this opportunity REAL (that is, is it likely to happen, or just imagined?). Does it merit the investment of the energy it will require? Or, does it have the odor of a pipe dream or mirage?

Secondly, is it a scenario where you can WIN? Is this a game or opportunity that you are capable of winning after giving your very best efforts? In other words, if you do all the right things, can you accomplish what you set out to do? (Remember in business, the rules of the poker table aren't always acceptable when you are essentially the trustee of other people's time and money. As a manager you must always know your capital tolerances and understand that the game of business isn't always based on winner take all.)

Finally, after you have your target in hand and have snagged that elusive account or acquisition, in the end will it have been WORTH the energy and effort expended? (Remember, energy is a valuable and increasingly priceless commodity.)

I admit that buying the Globetrotters was a very large risk and leap of faith. I had to put a career of 20-plus years on the line, along with most of my family's hard-earned liquidity. I was entering into a new but increasingly saturated industry, and I had to create new business networks, relationships and partnerships with many people I'd never worked with before. Most dauntingly, the company was extremely unhealthy and in the late stages of a bad bankruptcy. All of this was compounded by a post-market brand, not to mention the fact that I was Black and the first of my race to enter the world of sports and entertainment as an owner. Yet even in the most conservative restorative models, the skills required played to my business strength and training: I was physically and mentally prepared for a marathon effort, and the insights I had acquired over 40 years earlier from Abe Saperstein were still valid. Everyone I respected said that the projected returns on investment could best be achieved by someone with my unique background as both a business leader and former player. Win or lose, the social cause opportunity alone would balance the risk, secure my legacy, and give "risk-taking" confidence to those who came after me.

It's amazing the number of efficiencies you discover when you test your honesty and evaluate investments and opportunities in the real world. Before you make the financial and emotional plunge, ask yourself: Real, win, worth? Chances are that you will instantly know the answers.

Play Within Yourself, Play To your Strength

Over the years, I've developed a reputation for not over-reaching, for not over-rushing, for staying within the confines of my capabilities, and for not being greedy. These traits can be traced to my upbringing. Grandfather Jackson emphasized the danger of wanting too much out of a transaction or a relationship. From him I learned that greed and craving often cause the best of us to step outside our performance zone. It's helpful to start every task with the questions, "Who am I and what are my real intentions?" It's always helpful in building trust to be as transparent as possible.

To avoid over-reaching, you must first determine the status of your physical skills and mental and emotional capacities. That doesn't mean these traits can't be expanded through experience and additional knowledge, but it's essential to have a feel for your actual intentions and capabilities at any given time, especially if you are risking your future financial health or testing stories to attract other people's money. Critical attributes are energy, passion, intelligence and, most importantly, a willingness to put in the time. Confront your inner self with the question, "Am I playing to my real or perceived strengths?" You'll instantly receive the answer.

My father often talked about not outrunning your headlights. This is another way of saying, "If you go beyond your field of vision, bad things usually happen." Work on the things that increase your field of vision (like health, experience, education and good intentions). I was passionate about the Globetrotters, I knew early on what my intentions were, and I was willing to do whatever it took once I made the commitment. I also knew that the identifiable risks were manageable with minimal to no downside.

Be a Giver, Not a Taker

Giving, rather than taking, was another family-mandated value. Grandfather Jackson told me early in life that civilization is comprised of givers and takers and it was important to determine which I was going to be.

There was no doubt as to his preference. "We Jacksons have been blessed to have virtually the best of everything God could give a man or woman," he said. "Look around this neighborhood and at every member of the family. We have always prided ourselves on being available for others." Then he added, "When the world advances to a point where most people consider themselves givers, we'll have a much better neighborhood."

Have a Positive, Can-Do Attitude

I find that a positive attitude is vital for energizing yourself and your workplace. I'm not talking about being unrealistic; I'm just talking about practical optimism. A good attitude becomes contagious. It always acknowledges the possibility of success. It can also be a self-fulfilling prophecy. Shooting a basketball was never a problem for me, because I never doubted my ability. Conversely, for all the practice I've had and all the years I've played the game of golf, to this day the one constant in my game is doubt. At most I should be a 3 or 4 handicap. So when I retire I will practice much less, and focus exclusively on my attitude and belief system in order to build a more positive attitude toward my being a leader in the game.

In times of crisis, I tend to look for opportunity. My CEO at Honeywell, Ed Spencer, would often stress that a down market was the best time to invest. When competition is having problems, that's maybe not the time to reap profits. Market share and relationships are great investments in difficult times. Think about it. The healthy neighbor who never answers the phone or door appreciates a friendly visit when their health fails.

Each of us has the ability to decide what we want our life to become, and then design a process for reaching the desired outcome. Corporations call this visioning and strategic planning. In your personal life, it's simply saying you're taking control of where you'll go as well as the outcome you desire.

Professional speakers like to say that the road to success is one that is always under construction. But first, make sure the road you take has the assumed and desired destination.

With a little thought and a little assistance, a 15-year-old should be able to write today the resume he or she hopes to submit 30 years from now. The path to that outcome and each step along the way will say more about the quality of your life and your happiness than the destination.

Define and Redefine Success

Once you've decided not to be a victim, but rather to be the architect of your dreams and of your life's outcome, then it's important to develop realistic milestones, or success stops, that allow you to pause and make intelligent course adjustments. I recommend small steps, clearly defining each one before you undertake it. Once you complete each early step, you'll recognize your weaknesses and be encouraged by your successes.

The greatest company leaders, with a mantra of grow or die, learn about growth and long-range planning out of necessity, as they also discover the value of viewing the road to success as a continuum, thus taking a longer view of their wins and losses. The smart leader will also acknowledge the possibility of failures along the way and create recovery plans for setbacks as a part of the overall process. The creation of milestones allows you to test your assumptions and to make course corrections. The result is increased knowledge and the ability to apply that wisdom as the journey continues.

Take Care of Mind and Body

This is the most vital of the lessons I've learned, and no one can do it for you. Your mind and body must serve you a long time, often under stressful situations and frequently working without stopping for extended periods of time. Thus, your game plan for life must include a vision of how you're going to prepare yourself to maintain much-needed health and the competence to compete and win under pressure without risking your personal well-being. A part of anyone's readiness in this area is genetic makeup. However, there is a large part of your health you can control through diet and exercise, and through activities like yoga or meditation that focus the mind and body on healing and reflection. Each of these requires discipline and commitment.

Philosophies of moderation and preparation are absolutely necessary for a healthy professional lifestyle. Long ago, I made the decision to physically prepare for affairs of business as I would for a professional sport. I avoided alcohol, and while not adopting a complete vegan or vegetarian diet, I avoided red meat, sugar, excess sodium and dairy products. I used a regimen of diet and exercise to maintain my weight at its most optimum level. With at least eight hours of sleep I felt, all things being equal, like a well-conditioned athlete who has the best chance to win consistently.

Studies continue to show the subjective bias customers and employers have for physically fit, well-groomed professionals. Studies also show objective and empirical data on the enhanced longevity and on the high quality of work of these same professionals. I made the decision in the world of work, as I did in the world of sports, to stay in shape and remain healthy and prepared. I made taking care of mind and body my first order of business. Finally – and very importantly – I surrounded myself with like-minded individuals.

Life Really Is A Game

I have learned to approach life's events and crises in a strategic and calm manner. I never allow myself to confuse calm with denial: I just refuse to wallow in negative possible outcomes. Being focused and calm is easier when you have an ability to smile during crisis or confrontation. Seeing the humorous side of things whenever possible helps me manage tension. Managing the problems of the Harlem Globetrotters became a piece of cake as I learned to smile and enjoy the levity in this very complex and serious business.

Setbacks are best viewed as lessons that set the stage for future wins. Random acts of misfortune should be met with a brief counting of one's blessings followed by immediate attention to post-recovery – or, as we say in basketball, to the next shot.

In business, I see each decision not as a career-threatening burden, but as just another event in the bigger game to be mastered and enjoyed. With this attitude, it's amazing how much easier work becomes and how much easier it is for people to work with you.

Life is a collection of managing strategies and tactics, setting goals, developing alternative directions, measuring milestones, understanding the barriers, building quality metrics and trying to be the best you can be. Aren't these also elements we identify with our favorite games? Relax.

* * *

Everyone has their own particular philosophy as well as particular concerns that have arisen through unique upbringing, education and experience of the human condition. Some of your own ways of looking at the world are likely to overlap with the things on my list; some of my "words of wisdom" are things you may never have seriously considered. My list works for me because the items on it are linked to my causative reality.

Over time, one's operating behavior becomes much like one's fingerprint or DNA. It is an inextricable part of one's identity. So, take time to make a list of your own operating principles. And ask yourself: Are you happy? Are your behaviors working for you and, if not, what would you change? Then – and this is the critical part – make those changes. Dreams can become reality, but please don't count on it happening by luck or happenstance. They do so when we make the most of what we're given, keep our eye on the ball, work really hard – and more often than not, prepare yourself to give whatever it takes.

MANNIE JACKSON

EPILOGUE

In many ways my life has been so blessed simply because it changes, but the changes it presents sometimes challenge my strongest intentions and cause me to assess my priorities. When the unanticipated occurs, we are forced to weigh the responsibilities we feel to ourselves with those we feel toward others. Then and only then are we able to evaluate our preparation and readiness to face what life has placed in our path. The most prudently led lives allow room to mentally, emotionally and physically handle the forces of unexpected change.

In my own life, I've had to deal for so long with the issue of race. I have come to the realization that there are many issues and challenges in life significantly more profound and impactful that have absolutely no regard for race, gender, age or class. These changes and challenges often strike without prejudice.

As I navigated my life through a sometime hostile world, my life lesson is that we only own this moment. When the proverbial bell rings, one's readiness for change may be tested at any time as it introduces events and challenges beyond one's wildest dreams. It's only then that we will know and understand the depths of our true beliefs and emotional strengths. I've had my own readiness tested recently and I am not yet on the other side, but I can say that when it involves a family member and someone you love deeply, the test can be intense.

In this realm, over time, we eventually come to know the uncertainties we fear the most, and we also eventually discover that all of life's changes and outcomes are uncertain to a point. We are often forced to recognize the illusion of control we all face in our life journey, understanding that we travel an unknown road ahead.

Yet there is still so much we are empowered to do. As a mutually supportive and loving family of the universe, our skills to handle change can be honed. As my wife Cathy has repeated to me many times over these last few months, we must live calmly and preparedly, regularly celebrate the gift of friendships, cherish our earthly blessings, and remember to share them with others in need and listen to our guides. The lasting lesson for me will be: Life is less about the certainty of where we are going than about how we conduct ourselves along the way.

It is with love and appreciation that I dedicate this book, good health and happiness to my courageous wife and partner, who has chosen to tolerate and endure so much change, uncertainty and personal pain to keep our family as one.

It seems that Cathy and I are always on the go - and loving it.

A role model, leader, and friend - University of Illinois President - Dr. Joseph White. 2008

Dreams do come true.
The first African-American Chairman of the Naismith Memorial Basketball Hall of Fame Board of Trustees. 2005

Jay Leno - A great person and easy to be with. You wonder how someone so talented would work so hard and be so down-to-earth.

We tried to recruit MC Hammer as a producer and investor. We got something better - his friendship.

Abe Saperstein (Hall of Famer) Founder of sports' greatest brand. I liked the way he handled our relationship. 1962

Jackson Named Illinois Prep Player of Year:
Earlier in the month he was the highest vote getter for All-State's Honors, assuming the states mythical title Mr. Basketball. Shown Joe Lucco, Mannie Jackson, Mother and Father Margaret and Emmett Jackson and coach Dick Hutton.

Prince Charles - One of the world's most gifted and committed contributors.
I love telling about our 48-hour marathon experience of goodwill London, England.

One of the most fascinating days of my life. (60,000+ people, St. Peters Square) Pope John Paul II Named an honorary
Harlem Globetrotter.

Always available by phone - An amazingly brilliant thinker and communicator; who happens to have a lifetime contract with The Harlem Globetrotters. Bill Cosby. 2004

Giving back to youth at the Univ. Of Illinois - Over 1000 students are on track to be their best, over-come obstacles and help others thanks to Program Director Sheri Shaw, M.E. (Bottom Left) and Dean Tanya Gallager PHD. (Top Row Right) Shaw and Gallager are founders of the Mannie L. Jackson Illinois Academic Enrichment and Leadership Program.

The very proud Grandfather, three months before his death with Candace.
We all loved him and he'll stay in our memories. 2011

Jessie Jackson has created so much for so many, as a brilliant and tireless public servant.
A friend since our days at the University of Illinois. 2005

Maybe the best high school team in Illinois history. Five Div I players.

In South Africa every day started and ended with a press conference.

When Abe Saperstein put me on this great team my life changed.
Back Row: Tex Harrison, Sterling Forbes, JC Gipson, Willie Thomas, Murphy Summons
Front: Saperstein, Mannie Jackson, Meadowlark Lemon, Hallie Bryant, Parnell Woods

Ken "Buzz" Shaw, Don Gunther, Gov. Vaughn, Mannie Jackson, Lee May, Sam Johnson, and Harold Patton
This combination never lost a single game!

Mannie with the Godmother of our first born Candace and wife of Honeywell President Bob Rose. Alice Rose Helping out in South Africa

With Gov Vaughn, a great teammate and friend. In the opinion of many the best pure shooter and defensive player in Illinois history.

Shooting the jump shot from long range and running the floor came naturally after hours of practice.

A proud moment with the women in my life. The wedding of Candace -
With Mom Cathy and Sister Cassandra looking on.

I've watched him grow into a very special adult. It's nice when your son is a friend and favorite golf partner.

Mannie with his Dad and Sister Marjorie. 2008

General Colin Powell - A major force and leader.

With my Marjorie, I've been blessed to have had the love of someone so focused and supportive.

After all these years - I still love the game. Great performers like Curley "Boo" Johnson make it special.

One of the greatest leaders in the history of sports. Has always been objective and supportive.
David Stern - Commissioner NBA

Globie (Globetrotter Mascot) and South African youth.

A pair of MJ's reunite at The University of Illinois.

If you've never seen a railway boxcar, imagine this as a home for 14 in the Jackson - White Family in Illmo, Missouri.

This is what a railroad labor crew looked like in the 1930s and 40s.
My Grandfather in Illmo, Missouri was a "Straw Boss" for a group like this.

Jan and John Lenihan the parents of Executive assistant and the company's
Sr. Vice President of Sales and Marketing - Colleen Lenihan Olsen

The San Diego NBA Brain Trust....From Left - Richard Esquinas, Harry Cooper, Mannie Jackson, Alan Page, Attorney and
Strategist Ed Garvey (Founder NFL PLayers Association).

One of my greatest mentors, teachers, and inspirations. Every athlete needs a Coach Joe Lucco in their lives.

Sharing the stage with All-time great.
Northwest Airlines 50th Anniversary Celebration.

The fabled Dick Clark leads group to produce weekly TV show.

Mark Cuban - He's rich, he's loyal, he's passionate, and you can trust him.
One of the most interesting owners that's happen to sports in the last 50 years.

"Magic" just gets it! Talk about the "it" Factor. He's personable, smart and very loyal (Also a lifetime Harlem Globetrotter) One of my top 3 players of all time.

My wife Cathy getting her Masters Degree from Suffolk University in Boston, Mass.

"Red" Klotz...One of the game's greatest contributors. Known around the world as a leader and pioneer.

One of the greatest players the game has ever known. One of the greatest Globetrotter ever.
NBA legend Connie Hawkins with Mannie and Tex Harrison.

The Globetrotters: frequent visitors to network morning shows
Pose with Bryant Gumble and Kattie Couric.

A visit to Hollywood with Magic and Dennis Hopper.

Let's make another movie - A genius and icon with tons of "Street Cred". Adam Sandler

Chad Groth with icon Frederic "Curly" Neal

Gary Coleman..... Do you think he is a Globetrotter?

Charles Barkley.... No one better. He is the authentic Real Deal.

Receiving U of I Letterman achievement award in Edwardsville
Friends – Bill Penelton, Herman Shaw and Ed Lore - 2009

My sister Marjorie and mom Margaret.

1999 on Today Show with Globetrotter Entertainment legends:
Mike "Wildthing" Wilson, Hubert "Geese" Ausbie, Frederic "Curly" Neal, Matt "showbiz" Jackson "Sweet" Lou Dumbar

Legend and mentor Tex Harrison.